how to start a home-based

Editorial Services Business

HOME-BASED BUSINESS SERIES

how to start a home-based

Editorial Services Business

Barbara Fuller

Guilford, Connecticut

To Kevin, Kristina, Alicia, and Anthony—
for making it all possible and wonderful.

And to the members of Editcetera—
also for making it all possible and wonderful.

To buy books in quantity for corporate use
or incentives, call **(800) 962-0973**
or e-mail **premiums@GlobePequot.com.**

Editorial Director: Cynthia Hughes Cullen
Editor: Tracee Williams
Project Editor: Lauren Brancato
Text Design: Sheryl P. Kober
Layout: Casey Shain

Library of Congress Cataloging-in-Publication Data is available on file.
ISBN 978-0-7627-7882-9

Printed in the United States of America
10 9 8 7 6 5 4 3 2 1

Contents

Acknowledgments

I thank the many members of Editcetera who provided me with information about their experiences developing a freelance editorial career and working with clients through the years. I especially thank the following members, who took the time to answer questions directly about their experiences or contribute other input: Ariel Adams, Barbara Armentrout, Nancy Bell, Christopher Bernard, Mary Calvez, Catherine Cambron, Samuel Case, Juliet Clark, Geneviève Duboscq, Theresa Duran, Irene Elmer, Vicki Hammond, Janine Hannel, Bonnie Hupton, Brian Jones, Susan Ledford, Naomi Lucks, Beverly McGuire, Susan Moxley, Rebecca Pepper, Karen Seriguchi, David Sweet, and Loralee Windsor. Other members of the editing community to provide valuable input included John Bergez, Claire Chun, Marilyn Schwartz, and Stephanie Tanaka. I am fortunate to work in a community of smart and congenial editors and hope that the experiences shared here will help others attempting to work in this field.

I also thank Tracee Williams and Lauren Brancato of Globe Pequot Press for their guidance and support in this project.

Introduction

I was one of the lucky ones: From the time I was six years old, I knew what I wanted to do in life. I was going to be a writer. I had already written my first short story, everyone loved it, and I was on my way.

Through the years, I kept to that path—sort of. As I continued through elementary school, I wrote short stories whenever I could, sometimes illustrating them elaborately with a crayon. In my high school years, I packed my schedule with English classes: journalism, literature, writing, speaking . . . as many as I could take and still meet the other requirements of my school district and my parents. In college at Northwestern University, I started in journalism but shifted in my junior year to the more general Writing Program in the College of Arts and Sciences. Then it was on to grad school at UC Davis, with more writing. I studied fiction, taught fiction, loved fiction—but kept the general discipline of "writing."

I was learning, too, that what had started as a passion for writing was really a basic passion for words. It wasn't necessarily a matter of creating content; what I loved was making writing clear, getting it to convey original intentions in the best way possible. I shifted to working increasingly with the words of others. That work, whether developing an effective structure for a book or nitpicking at commas and capital letters, was editing.

Sound familiar? Many of you reading this book have probably experienced at least some aspects of the same interest in words. Others might have come through more roundabout channels, perhaps focusing on other subject matter (science? history? music?) and only later discovering that your real interest was in working with information about that discipline. And then, at some point, you realized that working with words itself interested you, even if the words weren't related to your original subject of interest.

Whatever the path, many of us with this love of words have faced the problem of how best to put our passion to work. Although staff positions exist for word lovers—many of them rewarding and prestigious jobs—much of the work exists outside the traditional nine-to-five world. And for some of us, work outside that world is even more appealing. The trick is to set up successfully from a home-based office.

Setting Out on My Own

Again, I was one of the lucky ones. Straight out of grad school, I landed a job as an editorial assistant at a choice publisher in my choice location, Sierra Club Books in San Francisco. I wasn't writing, and in fact, I was hardly editing. I was answering phones, typing letters (on a typewriter, with carbon paper and correction fluid when necessary), and filing (still not one of my greater talents). Occasionally I got to communicate with an author, or proofread a late chapter, or write a blurb for a jacket or a catalog.

It was enough to hook me; I loved this business of publishing. But the key here was "occasionally." I was fortunate to have smart and encouraging bosses at the Sierra Club, but this entry-level staff job simply didn't offer much opportunity to edit. Looking back, I now know how valuable that two-year introduction to publishing was for me, and I would encourage anyone starting in the business to snag such an opportunity. But I soon itched to move up, and then I began to see that even if I did move up, I might spend more time shepherding manuscripts and attending meetings than actually editing. I had discovered the joy in editing—a curve from the writing ambition I had as a six-year-old—but I didn't see much editing ahead on staff, either.

After a brief stray into magazine work, where I did find more hands-on editing as well as writing, I decided to give the freelance world a try. I was pregnant with my first child and liked the idea of flexibility paired with satisfying work. Although San Francisco is no New York when it comes to publishing, we have quite a few book publishers in our area, and I set about firing off cover letters and résumés in search of work. It took me many years to learn of the abundance of other editorial opportunities for freelancers in my area, too, from the relatively high-paying tech editing projects in the Silicon Valley to corporate publications, advertising brochures, nonprofit publications, and university reports in every discipline. As Internet communications swept the world, with new web content as well as e-publications for books that had formerly been distributed only in hard copy, more opportunities opened.

And as authors with all kinds of subject matter and levels of expertise discovered self-publishing, they too realized a need for editors even as they skirted traditional publishing.

So yes, work for word lovers abounds. The problem is in finding that work, getting the potential client to hire you, and then getting the existing client to hire you again. Balancing the inconsistent flow of work with a personal life and maintaining financial stability add to the challenge.

Even with all problems considered, I have never regretted taking that scary jump from the security of employment. It's been twenty-two years since I first inquired meekly about freelance opportunities with a local publisher, and I'm still in the world of home-based editing. Some of this time I have been engaged full-time in freelance work from my home office, contributing my share to the family income solely from an assortment of freelance projects. Other years have been divided between my own freelance work and my work as director of Editcetera, an association of one-hundred-plus freelancers based in Berkeley, California.

Sometimes, as I manage Editcetera, I am thankful for my life now, free of the uncertainty of self-employment, of the anxiety over what might be next and the aggravation of working with sometimes difficult clients. But many times I envy those who still count on their home-based business full-time—who have an ongoing influx of exciting new projects, who find fascinating and intelligent clients to constantly challenge them, and who can close the office door every now and then just because they want to without consulting a vacation calendar.

Using This Book

Whether you have begun your career on staff in publications and want to start a home-based business, or you hope to make a shift from another career, or you intend to moonlight while you continue a related career (perhaps in journalism or teaching), this book will help you set up for success. Chapters 1 through 4 will help you get started and plan your business; chapters 5 and 6 address money matters; and chapters 7 through 9 focus on marketing and client relations. Chapters 10 (legal and ethical issues), 11 (balancing business and family), and 12 (building and expanding your business) address other important concerns.

In chapter 1, "Making the Decision," you'll read about the pros and cons of running a home-based business so you can make an informed decision about whether this career move is right for you. Chapter 2, "Envisioning the Business," will help you define your niche and set up the business that works best for you. Chapter 3, "Setting Up Your Home Office," will guide you through considerations regarding physical space, and chapter 4, "Getting Started," introduces you to the details of registering your business and developing a business plan.

Editors aren't always savvy about money matters and other business particulars, but you must consider these issues carefully if you want to succeed as a freelancer. Chapter 5, "Managing Finances," gives advice on setting rates and getting paid. "Keeping Records and Paying Taxes," chapter 6, gives you tools for tracking your money and staying in good favor with the IRS.

Marketing and maintaining clients is key to any successful home business. Chapter 7, "Connecting with Clients," is full of tips for locating potential clients and persuading them to hire you. "Using the Internet," chapter 8, goes into details about this essential tool of the twenty-first century. Finally, after you have set up your business and landed some work, you'll want to keep your clients happy so they come back to you if they have more work and refer you to their colleagues even if they don't. Chapter 9, "Working with Clients," addresses these issues and also includes tips for working with (or discontinuing work with) difficult clients.

Formal contracts aren't always necessary for editorial projects, but you'll want some sort of written agreement in place to avoid potential trouble. You'll also want to consider ethical issues as you choose your clients; your reputation is going to be your biggest asset as you build your business. Chapter 10, "Sizing Up Legal and Ethical Issues," introduces some of these issues for consideration to help you work responsibly.

Chapter 11, "Balancing Business and Family," is for the many home-based editors who juggle a career with family responsibilities. Many editors, in fact, make the transition to freelancing specifically with this goal in mind. If this is your situation, firm guidelines can help you succeed in both areas of life. If this is not your situation, you might be trying to balance other priorities: maybe volunteer work or even another career. Then, too, this chapter might give you some insight. If you are committed foremost to your editorial business, skip chapter 11—at least for now.

If you have set up your business but want to build your clientele or increase your hourly rate, think about ways to improve your marketability. Chapter 12, "Developing and Expanding Your Business," gives suggestions for building on your existing set of skills, gaining experience, and branching out into related fields.

If you are a talented wordsmith, and if you develop your business wisely, you will have choices in your home-based career. Plan carefully and set yourself up right, and you could share the rewarding work and lifestyle that so many of your word-loving colleagues enjoy.

Do You Really Want to Be a Home-Based Editor?

In my home region of the San Francisco Bay Area, publishing is relatively big business. It's not as big here as in New York, but opportunities abound for those who look for them. With thirty-eight publishers listed for San Francisco in the 2012 edition of *Literary Market Place (LMP)*, and with more in the nearby cities, we are putting out plenty of books.

Add to those books a handful of magazines also published in my area, and the word count rises. Then add numerous trade journals, government reports, and university publications, and you see the demand. Outside of traditional publishing and publications, we find a need for editors to work on everything from documentation associated with the tech industry of the Silicon Valley to the small-print literature packed in medications sold over the counter. Since the 1990s, we have also seen a profusion of print on the web and an influx of self-published works by everyone from grandfathers publishing memoirs to business executives broadcasting their expertise. More and more people are writing—and many of these people value the editor's professional eye.

This is my home ground, the San Francisco Bay Area—one of the bigger publishing centers of the country but not close to the top. Take those thirty-eight publishers in San Francisco and multiple by ten, and you start to approach what New York City holds. Throughout the country, according to *LMP* listings, more than twenty-five hundred publishers are hard at work producing pages. Many of these publishers have always counted on freelancers to meet their needs for proofreading, copyediting, and indexing. Some also depend on freelancers to provide other editorial services, such as development or production. And publishers publish only a small share of the material that goes into print every day; self-publishing, print-on-demand, and the World Wide Web are other means of production and distribution.

You see the point. There's a lot of work. The problem? Working with words appeals to many, many people, including English majors as well as other word lovers who have developed a skill through a variety of channels. You won't find "editing" listed in university catalogs as an undergraduate degree, yet educated people of many disciplines claim the profession. According to the US Labor Department, "Strong competition is expected for salaried editing jobs because many people want to work in the media industry."[1] So the facts are (1) US businesses publish a lot of words, (2) a lot of those words need editors, (3) a lot of people want to edit those words, and (4) staff jobs are relatively scarce.

The good news is that many businesses—publishers and others alike—continue to recognize the need for a good editor to make communications clear even if they don't hire editors on staff. These businesses look for talented freelancers, and while some ask freelancers to work on-site in makeshift cubicles when needed, many send work over the Internet for completion at a remote office. Even if you don't live in a publishing hub like New York City—or in a community with a single publisher listed in the Yellow Pages—you can still get work over the Internet. Well-established freelancers in rural areas of Middle America can stay busy with clients from afar, and even some who have moved temporarily outside the national boundaries have maintained their US clients. As of 2012, 16 percent of all editors were self-employed, and that rate is expected to remain stable through 2020, according to the US Department of Labor/Employment and Training Administration.[2]

So plenty of work is available specifically for home-based editors. But just as for staff jobs, many editors want that home-based work. This means that only those with the sharpest skills *and the best and most professional business practices* get the work. Many editors do make a comfortable living from a home office; some are able not only to pay their bills but to choose the jobs that most appeal to them. But those editors haven't happened into that success; they have worked hard for it, and they have been smart about how they developed their business. Other wannabe freelance

1 US Department of Labor, Bureau of Labor Statistics, *Occupational Outlook Handbook,* 2012; www.bls.gov/ooh/media-and-communication/editors.htm, accessed September 25, 2012.
2 O*NET OnLine, www.onetonline.org/find/industry?j=27-3041.00&i=94, accessed September 25, 2012.

editors have given up—some because they didn't have the editorial skills and others because they didn't have the business know-how. The trick is to make yourself one of the many skilled *and* business-savvy editors who succeed.

If you persist and succeed, you will find a rewarding line of work. The decision now is whether you want the career and lifestyle that comes with it enough to do what it takes. If you are considering moving into freelance editing, make sure you know what that means. This chapter explores the pros and cons of home-based editorial work as well as the necessary qualities of a freelance editor.

Why Edit?

The first question to ask is whether you really want to edit at all. Do you love to work with words? Love to help bring out the best in writing—whether by shaping the manuscript as a whole or by nitpicking over every comma and hyphen until all are perfect? In chapter 2, "Envisioning the Business," we'll discuss types of editing that might appeal to you as well as different types of publications and potential clients. For now, let's assume you have already chosen the field of editing and are deciding whether to work out of your home as a freelancer.

> **Keep in Mind**
>
> The good news: People are always writing, and writing requires editing.
> The bad news: Competition for editorial work is fierce.

Why Freelance? The Pros

What exactly is a freelancer? A *freelancer* is a self-employed professional who provides services to a variety of clients without a long-term commitment to any of them; *freelancing* is providing this type of service. Often—but not always—freelancers work out of their homes, sometimes without ever meeting their clients face-to-face. People start freelancing for all kinds of reasons: some for their interest in working with a variety of clients, some because they want to combine editorial work with another life commitment, and some because they can't find other work that suits them.

Two things inspired me. First, I wanted to do hands-on editing and didn't have a good opportunity for staff work at the time that would allow me to do that. Second, I was pregnant with my first child, and I wanted to keep working but avoid the constraints of a nine-to-five office job. I didn't think as seriously beyond those two objectives as I might have or as I would encourage you to do. I had an editor-mentor from my former employer, Sierra Club Books, who suggested I read *The Chicago Manual of Style* (yes, all six-hundred-plus pages of the thirteenth edition), and that turned out to be good advice. She also gave me some freelance work and some suggestions for other avenues to tap. Beyond that, I muddled through. With this book, I hope to reduce the amount of muddling necessary for others.

Why do other editors set up a home-based business? "Primarily to work at home and organize my time as I prefer, as long as I meet the clients' deadlines," says one established freelancer, summing up what many value most. Other editors cite the following motivators for turning to home-based work:

- an ability to focus more on editing with fewer distractions
- a desire to apply language skills in a new way
- a desire to apply teaching skills in a new way
- exposure to a wide variety of subjects
- a frequent change of projects and assignments
- the diversity of clients and their subject matter
- an ability to get paid to read interesting and informative text
- an ability to work at home in the evenings
- an ability to work while waiting for the kids at soccer practice or drama rehearsal
- an ability to work hard for a time and then not at all
- an ability to dress without worry about others' expectations
- an ability to schedule other activities during the day
- an ability to work with a child at home
- freedom from work in a traditional office
- freedom from office meetings
- freedom from office politics
- freedom from a commute
- an ability to enhance skills as desired
- an ability to supplement income
- independence

Many of these advantages are self-explanatory. Some merit further discussion, however. These fall more or less into five categories: a flexible lifestyle, control over the means of doing work, a variety of work, freedom from office politics, and an opportunity for growth.

A Flexible Lifestyle

I recently asked a colleague if she could take a job that needed to be done on a particular day. No, she said, she could not. She wanted to make reservations to take a Grand Canyon river-rafting trip with her family and needed to sit at her computer as long as necessary to make the online reservation. I couldn't imagine someone in a staff job taking a vacation day just to book a vacation, yet I knew that Internet reservations for high-demand adventures often require persistence. This colleague, a freelancer, was able to shift hours as she liked. She had built a reputation among her clients and had as much work as she wanted. Furthermore, her clients probably didn't know that she was Internet-sitting; undoubtedly, they were happy with the work she sent to them on deadline that week. She just didn't want to be tied to an hour-sensitive job that particular day.

Are you a night owl who works best after dinner and can still be productive at 2:00 a.m.? With some qualifications—most important, the ability to communicate with clients during business hours—you can choose your hours. Want to volunteer as a docent for a local museum every Wednesday? Or work in your child's school library one morning a week? If you have the professional work to keep you busy and can't afford to cut your hours, just work a little extra late in the day or over the weekend. Need to spend a month with your aging parents in another state? Your client might not even know you have temporarily relocated.

Whether you want to work odd hours or irregular hours, whether you want to work from one convenient office or occasionally from others, the options are open. Without a clock to punch or a manager to sign you off, a home-based editor can pick the schedule that suits (within reason). After you have established yourself and can choose from your job offers, you can even pick the amount of work you do (and get paid to do)—full-time when your kids are in school or when you need a little extra cash for something or part-time when the rest of the family has time off or when you get a rare opportunity to join an alum group for a trip to Italy.

Control over Work

Closely related to flexibility is the issue of control: The stereotypical caricature of a freelancer is one sitting with slippered feet propped on a desk and with a cup of tea in hand. It's true that the freelancer need not dress for anyone in particular when working at home; the worker's wardrobe can be all about comfort and nothing about what anyone else thinks. No boss will determine what you do when, what music you play in the background, or whether the cat can sit at your feet (but beware: I've heard more than one horror story about a cat on a computer keyboard). The home-based editor's job is to get the work done—well and on time. You determine the means of doing that work.

Variety in Work

Throughout my college and grad school years, I had spent every summer working at camps or state parks. When I landed my first publishing job, Sierra Club Books seemed like a perfect place to combine my love of nature with my love of words. And when I left the Sierra Club to begin freelancing, environmentalism presented an ideal niche. It was a topic that interested me and one that I had learned a bit about. It was also something I wanted to keep learning about, and what better way to learn than to get paid to edit books about a subject?

Familiarity with subject matter can sometimes help convince a client that you are the right person to do a job. In general, though, editorial skills are more important than subject matter expertise. At different times in my career, I have worked in such diverse and interesting fields as history, politics, psychology, gardening, and microbiology. I have worked on cookbooks, children's books, and novels. For a while, I focused on software textbooks—a great way to earn some money while building my expertise with tools that would be useful throughout my career. For some types of editorial work (e.g., developmental editing), subject matter expertise is important. For other types (e.g., copyediting and proofreading), you don't need to know anything at all about the subject of your publication. But imagine being able to read and learn about so many different subjects—and get paid to do so.

For a long time after one of my daughters was born prematurely, I specialized in health care. I remember sitting in the neonatal intensive care unit next to my daughter's Isolette in awe of the nurses' work, grateful for their care. Briefly I considered changing careers and learning something about the all-important field of medicine. But then I realized that I could contribute to health care using my own existing set of skills and talents. Soon after, I began a long stint of freelance editorial work for *Neonatal Network* journal and for other health-related publications.

More recently, as the wife of a public school teacher and the mother of three children, my interest has shifted to education. Turn to teaching? No, I simply applied my editorial skills to new subject matter. For several years I specialized in education, working for one journal on the topic and directly for a couple of university professors of education. One of my most rewarding projects to date has been helping a university professor to present information clearly based on education research that seemed important to me. I learned as I worked and also felt the satisfaction of contributing silently to the field.

What's next? Maybe loving care for the elderly. I know editors who have moved into tech work after developing an interest and aptitude for computers or into fiction after developing a passion for novels. Others who started in book publishing found that they enjoyed the intensity (and often higher pay) of corporate work. The point is, we have choices. Working from a home-based office enables the freelancer to move from one type of publication to another, from one subject matter to the next.

An Absence of Office Politics

Drama in the workplace might be something you have learned to accept—or ignore. But for many who have worked as an employee, the freelancer's relief from politics is welcome. Alone in your own space, you need to respect your clients and to learn how to work successfully with them. You do not need to worry about which fellow employee has what office or who got a promotion that someone else deserved. You worry about the job at hand and do it to the best of your ability. That's all.

Opportunity for Growth

If you have ever had a job where you knew you could do more challenging and interesting work but were constrained by the routine tasks of your job description, you will value the ability to manage your own self-growth. As a freelancer, you control not only the means of your work but also the development of your career. If you want to build new skills, figure out which ones are important to you, and take a relevant course or find a good self-help book. If you want to take on more work, take it on. You might need to do more marketing at first rather than more paid editing, but figure out what avenues you want to explore, and explore them. You are the chief decision maker in your business, so make the decisions that will lead you where you want to go.

Why Not Freelance? The Cons

If all of the news about freelancing were good, there would be far too many free-lance editors in the world and far too little work to share among us. In reality, there are downsides as well, and anyone considering work as a freelancer needs to think about whether these downsides are worth the upsides. Five issues in particular deserve consideration from anyone anticipating a move to a home-based business: the concept of feast and famine, a lack of control over time, temperamental clients, a lack of community, and a lack of benefits. You might notice that some of these cons seem opposite some of the pros just discussed. (See "Pros and Cons of Freelancing.") You are right.

Pros and Cons of Freelancing

Pros	Cons
A flexible lifestyle	A life of feast and famine
Control over work	A lack of control over time
Variety in work	Temperamental clients
An absence of office politics	A lack of community
Opportunity for growth	A lack of benefits

A Life of Feast and Famine

One of the most important things to understand about operating a home-based business is the concept of feast and famine, of too much work one day and too little the next. In the beginning, famine will probably predominate. When you begin a new job as an employee, you start earning a paycheck immediately, even if you accomplish little during your first days (or weeks or more). When you are self-employed, however, you might get little if any pay in the beginning, even if you are hard at work setting up, learning what you need to know, and searching for clients.

If you are persistent (and at least a little bit lucky), you might land a job soon—maybe on the Wednesday before Thanksgiving, when your dream client cannot find anyone else to take a job. Work through Thanksgiving? How much do you want the job? Perhaps you get another call on the Friday after Thanksgiving from another client you have been prospecting for months. Not only is your Thanksgiving weekend gone now, but so are the weeks leading up to Christmas or Hanukah or some other occasion that most people consider sacred. Gone are your days for shopping and decorating. After waiting and worrying about how you will make ends meet through September and October, this might seem unfair. But as a beginning freelancer, you feel you must accept the work. If you want to succeed, you might be right. Forgetting their own early days, seasoned freelancers might warn you to set boundaries—but you will probably need to work whenever you can at first, even if that means taking too much work at times to balance too little at other times. Just how flexible are you, and how willing to overload yourself when the work is available?

As you develop your business and build your clientele, ideally you will get to a place where you do not need or want to accept every job offer. Even the most established among us, however, still have slow moments and other times that are busier than we would like. One of the most frustrating aspects of freelancing, says editor Christopher Bernard, can be "the long, unplanned breaks that sometimes happen between projects, which result in a lower annual income than [one] would like." A beginner's life? No. Christopher has been a successful freelancer for nearly thirty years, and his experience is common.

Advice from a Freelancer

"Don't assume that you'll always stay as busy as you are in your busiest periods. Slow periods will come, sometimes unexpectedly, and sometimes they'll last for weeks or months."—Brian Jones, Freelance Editor

Managers for book publishers and corporations alike often depend on freelancers to adjust to meet schedules, to wait (without pay) when a schedule slips and then to overwork when a project is behind. The trick is to hoard during periods of feast and to work on developing your business during times of famine. If you are able to manage both your money and your time through these cycles, you will do well. If you lack the discipline or the heart for this, you might want to stick with a nine-to-five staff job.

A Lack of Control over Time

When we discussed the positive aspects of freelancing, we talked about control. But the need to take jobs when they come, at least in the beginning, can overshadow control. Remember that job that arrived just before Thanksgiving? You might feel completely out of control as you realize you have bills to be paid and must now defer to others to cook the turkey. How much control you have depends on which clients you have developed and how successfully you have built your business. In the beginning, if you want to be paid, you might need to jump when you can.

Lessons Learned

Most editors begin a home-based business with the illusion that they will be able to control their own time all of the time. Most soon learn the reality. "Even though one of the appeals of freelancing is being able to set your own schedule," says freelance editor Juliet Clark, "I find that I frequently have to change my plans when clients don't meet their own deadlines, so in fact I have much less control over my time than I might like."

Temperamental Clients

While freelancers enjoy independence and freedom from answering to a regular boss, working with the revered variety of clients also means dealing with a variety of temperaments. Many clients are professional, intelligent, pleasant, and grateful for help from a skilled freelancer, but others are less knowledgeable about the business and less patient with the process. Editors need to remember that a manuscript can be very personal, almost an extension of the self, and even someone who asks for help might be sensitive and argumentative when the help is offered. Especially without the support of a professional colleague in the next cubicle, the situation can be stressful.

A Lack of Community

While many home-based editors value the absence of office politics, some miss the community involvement. If you enjoy having lunch with a colleague, catching up socially over a break, or even commuting in a carpool or on public transit, freelance work might not be for you. If you enjoy regular discussions with groups of people—if you look forward to office meetings and the face-to-face give-and-take at those meetings—you might be better off working on staff.

Home-based work does not need to be solitary. You should be communicating with others, sometimes by phone or e-mail discussion. You might participate in an occasional conference call or attend a live meeting, and you would do well to join a professional group if you can find one in your community. Some home-based editors also find work teaching and develop a social community that way. But the ratio of professional other-people time to alone time will be relatively low if you work from your home. That temperamental client we discussed earlier? You might be on your own to decompress.

A Lack of Benefits

One of the most tangible disadvantages to working as a freelancer is the lack of benefits. Employees often take benefits for granted, but freelancers soon discover what they are missing.

- **Employer contributions to Social Security and Medicare.** Employers typically pay half of all Social Security and Medicare taxes for employees, while employees pay the other half directly. In most recent years, these taxes together have added up to 15.3 percent of an employee's wages. Self-employed workers must pay the same 15.3 percent themselves, without employer contribution. Thus a freelancer who makes $30,000 would pay $4,590 in Social Security and Medicare taxes, called self-employment taxes for them, rather than the $2,295 that an employee would pay.
- **Medical insurance.** As a freelancer, unless you share benefits provided for another family member, you will need first to find a health care provider who will accept you and then to pay your own premiums. Although changes to health care policy in our country are imminent, as of this writing, self-employed individuals with a pre-existing medical condition especially find it difficult to get insurance and the care they need. And while many employees rely on employer-provided dental and vision care, freelancers need to locate and pay for those services themselves.
- **Disability insurance.** Home-based business owners do not automatically get state-provided disability insurance. Although you might be able to obtain disability insurance through your state or from a private provider, you will need to pay for it out of pocket. If you work without this insurance, as many

freelancers do, you will risk a complete absence of income if you become seriously ill or have an accident, and you will have no maternity or family coverage in case of a birth.

- **Vacation days.** Yes, you can take as many vacation days as you like as a freelancer—but you won't be paid for those days. I know freelance editors who take off several months every year. But either those freelancers have been in business long enough to be very successful or they have other income to help them through the times without pay. Some home-based editors limit themselves to two weeks of unpaid vacation a year or never take a planned vacation at all.

- **Health days.** Loss of pay in times of illness is similar to loss of paid vacation days—except that you cannot plan ahead for illness. You won't be staying in bed with the security of a paycheck if you get the flu; you might just need to clear your head and get busy. If you are unable to complete a job on time, you could lose the work altogether, and if you do not yet have a solid reputation established with the client, you could lose the client. Your client in need of your help probably won't sympathize.

- **A retirement plan.** Although money-smart freelancers might set up an independent retirement plan and defer or avoid some tax payments through that plan, no employer will match your contribution; you will be on your own.

With planning, you can adjust and provide for your own needs. Appendix A, "Resources for Editors," lists groups that sometimes help freelancers obtain medical and disability insurance, for example. You will need to search and apply for the right programs, though, and then pay for them out of pocket. Many freelancers do this— but before you head into business for yourself, make sure you understand the value of the benefits sometimes taken for granted by employees.

Are You Right for Freelancing?

So now you've thought about the pros and cons of working independently in a home-based business. Maybe you have decided that yes, this is a career path you would like to pursue. The next question is, are you suited for this type of work?

Required Professional Skills

If you are not currently an editor but are considering entering the editorial business, make sure you have what it takes to do the job. You can build on your skills, as discussed throughout this book, but you should start with some basics, including the following:

- **A firm grasp of the English language.** You started learning to speak as a toddler and have developed proficiency through years of school and practice. A grammar class can help you work with some trickier aspects of the language, but if you don't have a good base to begin with, editing probably isn't for you.

- **An ear for language.** The English language is complex. While mastery of the rules is essential, a good editor also knows when to diverge. Voracious reading is one way to develop an ear that transcends the rules.

- **Knowledge of at least one style manual.** Editors need to know intimately at least one major style guide, determined by the type of work they do. Some of the most common guides are *The Chicago Manual of Style* (for books and many other publications), *The Associated Press Stylebook* (for journalism), *MLA Style Manual and Guide to Scholarly Publishing* (for scholarly work), *Publication Manual of the American Psychological Association* (also for scholarly work, especially in the behavioral and social sciences), *American Medical Association Manual of Style* (for medical publications), and *Microsoft Manual of Style* (for technical work). These guides work as references and do not need to be memorized, but good editors know what is in them and have mastered key points.

- **Attention to detail.** If you hope to copyedit, you should notice when seventeen on page 4 becomes 17 on page 24 and when that shift in style is correct; when de' Medici on page 19 is De Medici on page 400 and whether the variation is ever ok; and whether the word should be nonnative or non-native or non-Native. You should also notice whether a semicolon has been set in ital (;) or roman (;), and you should know which is correct. Not only should you know; you should care. If you don't know now, you should learn how to find out and find out quickly. If you don't care, you might find work doing some types of editing, but getting a start might be slow; those new to the business often find their first jobs as proofreaders or copyeditors, so ability to focus on details when necessary is important.

- **An ability to think analytically and logically.** Especially if you want to work as a developmental editor, you will need to be able to view a manuscript as a whole, in a broad sense, and figure out how to make it better.

- **An aptitude for basic computer work, including proficiency with Microsoft Word.** The computer will be your tool, fundamental to your business. Clients generally expect editors to have at least rudimentary computer skills, and the more proficient you are, the more marketable you will be.
- **A desire to learn.** As an editor, you will constantly need to question. If you are willing to glide over an illogical statement, you might not be the best editor. If you find yourself always searching for more, needing to understand, you are more likely to do well.

We'll talk more about specific qualifications for different types of editorial work in chapter 2, "Envisioning the Business."

Essential Interpersonal Characteristics

Although you might envision editing as a solitary act, it really is not; the editor's task is to help someone else accomplish a goal. In addition to having editorial skills, you will need the following personal and interpersonal characteristics:

- **Good judgment.** When do you insist on a change, and when do you let go? When do you ask questions, and how? An editor who never asks a question isn't thinking carefully enough. One who asks too many questions will irritate a client in need of help and short on time. Some discretion comes through experience. Some is common sense.
- **An ability to communicate tactfully with authors.** Editors are helpers; the whole point is to assist an author. And authors, even as they strive for per-

Getting It Right

Freelance editor Bonnie Hupton recalls a success she had with a potentially difficult client. "I edited a research paper by a researcher once," she says, "and he complained beforehand that he was a 'very good writer and didn't really *need* an editor.' But because it was [company] policy for published papers to go through the editing process, he had no choice. When I returned his paper he was so impressed he asked me to edit an article that he was going to submit to a magazine, and he paid me himself!"

fection, can be sensitive. If you offend your author, no matter how right you are in your criticism, you will fail. Practice will help you improve your communication skills, but a certain amount of tact should be inherent.

- **Stress tolerance.** Between tight deadlines, demanding clients, and sometimes critical authors, editing can be stressful. The freelancer needs the poise to shepherd projects calmly and diplomatically to success.

Mandatory Business Ability

Finally, no matter what small business you hope to operate, it will succeed only if you have some basic business skills, including the following:

- **Willingness and ability to market.** As a freelancer, you will have no guarantee for work beyond the job on your desk. Finding one job isn't enough; ongoing marketing will be essential.
- **An ability to manage time.** Especially during times of feast, you might seem to have more to do than you can possibly accomplish. You will be your own manager, responsible for finishing each project when promised. If you miss deadlines, word will travel fast, and work will slow if not stop.
- **An ability to manage money.** No accounting department will see that you get paid or ration out your money when you do. To work for yourself, you need both the acquired skills and the number sense to keep yourself in the black.
- **Self-discipline.** With the benefit of flexibility comes the need for discipline. If you can sleep in until 9:00 a.m., why not 10:00 a.m.? If you can take an hour off to work in your child's school library, why not another hour to watch a favorite television program? Can you ignore the solitaire game that too often comes preloaded on computers? Are you smart enough to remove the application if it's a problem? And if you can control the background music in your office, will you make sure it doesn't interfere with your work? No one will succeed at business without the discipline to do the work and do it well. If you need to clock in and out of work to make your hours, you will need to either build in some system for doing that or realize that you would do better with the structure of a staff job.
- **Patience with administrative tasks.** You won't find anyone to check your mail or send out your invoices; you'll be on your own. Administration has nothing to do with creating books, but it has everything to do with successful freelancing.

To measure your aptitude for freelance editorial work, complete the following self-assessment: "Do You Have What It Takes to Be a Freelance Editor?" If you lack some needed skills and characteristics and don't know how to build them, read on, and revisit the chart after you have finished this book.

Do You Have What It Takes to Be a Freelance Editor?

For each of the following characteristics of a home-based editor, check the box under "Have" if you think you are already proficient or under "Need" if you think you fall short of this skill. If you mark "Need," also jot some notes under "Strategy for Acquisition" about how you might obtain the skill. If you don't think you can acquire it or don't have a desire to do so, reconsider whether you should be starting a home-based editorial business.

Skill	Have	Need	Strategy for Acquisition
Professional Skills			
A firm grasp of the English language			
An ear for language			
Knowledge of at least one style manual			
Attention to detail			
An ability to think analytically and logically			
An aptitude for basic computer work, including proficiency with Microsoft Word			
A desire to learn			

Interpersonal Characteristics			
Good judgment			
An ability to communicate tact-fully with authors			
Stress tolerance			
Business Skills			
Willingness and ability to market			
An ability to manage time			
An ability to manage money			
Self-discipline			
Patience with administrative tasks			

Is Freelancing Right for You?

If you have read this far and determined that you have the skills to succeed in a home-based business or think you can develop them, consider next whether the lifestyle would work for you. It's not just about loving your work; it's about surviving.

Fit with Other Aspects of Your Life

Never mind your interest or good intentions. Do you have the self-discipline to make a home-based business successful? If you share a home with another adult, will that adult respect your business? Can you shut the door to your child if you have a deadline pending but no one to notice if you aren't at your desk? Is flexibility really something you desire, or do you need a more rigid schedule? If you think you can manage, read on.

Financial Reality

Think carefully about the bottom line. How much money do you need, and how soon? Yes, many freelancers earn a respectable living from their homes. Some earn a good living, in fact; an annual income in the six digits is even possible, especially for tech editors. But most must learn to live frugally, at least for a while. And few make enough to support themselves at all right away. Do you have another source of income while you build your business? Another part-time job? Some money squirreled away from past work? Maybe you have a spouse who can help support you for a while? If so, move on.

If not, don't give up—but do think about how you are going to hold things together while you build. We'll talk more about these issues in later chapters, but it's important to be realistic. Income could be small in the beginning. Be prepared—but know, too, that everyone starts somewhere. If the pros discussed at the start of this chapter appeal to you, if the cons seem surmountable, and if you meet or think you can meet all of the qualifications listed under "Are You Right for Freelancing?" move on. Start planning your business, and forge ahead.

02

Envisioning the Business

What Will You Do, and for Whom?

Now that you have decided you want to be in business for yourself, think about the skills that you can offer. Many readers of this book are probably coming from a background in journalism or publishing, but some might be teachers or other individuals with an interest in working with words. What skills do you have that you might apply to editing? What skills do you think you could acquire?

Defining Your Niche

If you have worked on staff in publishing, you already know how many different types of editorial work exist. If you have worked in the publications department of another type of business, you might have done a little bit of everything—from writing to proofreading and possibly even layout. To determine your goals, think about the different kinds of editorial services offered and which ones might be a fit for you. Also consider potential clients; different types of clients have different editorial needs for freelancers, as well as different content areas and (not to be ignored) different pay scales.

What Will You Do?

In this book, we discuss home-based editing that encompasses all of the various editorial skills—developmental editing, copyediting, production editing, and other variations. While designers and other production-oriented professionals are also in demand, they require different skills and are outside the boundaries of this book. Writers too are beyond the scope of this book. Here we focus on editorial tasks, including proofreading and indexing. For a summary of different types of editorial skills, see "Editorial Skills and Starting Rates." For a more comprehensive discussion, read on.

Note that I include here brief discussions of pay. Rates vary widely depending on the demands of the job and the skill of the freelancer. A beginning but skilled freelancer working for a nonprofit or an independent author can probably (but not definitely) make at least the minimum rates noted here. More experienced editors or those working on more difficult projects might make considerably more. For a detailed discussion of rates, see chapter 5, "Managing Finances," and appendix B, "Editorial Skills, Rates, and Paces." The comments here are intended only to give you a place to start in your thinking.

Editorial Skills and Starting Rates

Editorial Title	Brief Description	Typical Pay
Proofreader	Checks final pages for errors in text and design	$15/hour +
Copyeditor	Ensures correct use of language and consistent style—word for word and sentence for sentence	$20/hour +
Editorial proofreader	Performs a combination of proofreading and light copyediting tasks	$20/hour +
Substantive editor	Performs heavy-level copyediting tasks; rewrites for clarity and tone	$35/hour +
Developmental editor	Works with the author on broad issues of content and organization	$40/hour +
Technical editor	Ensures that difficult information is presented clearly; can include copyediting and/or developmental editing	$40/hour +
Fiction editor	Works with creative manuscripts, taking particular care to maintain the author's style; can include copyediting and/or developmental editing	$15/hour +
Web editor	Edits material for the web, utilizing knowledge of on-screen reading practices and search functions	$40/hour +
Indexer	Creates an alphabetical list of items within a text to help a reader navigate a publication	$30/hour +

Production editor	Manages publishing projects from manuscript to delivery of bound books	$40/hour +
Acquisitions editor	*Senior-level staff position:* finds the books and authors that a company will publish	Salaried
Managing editor	*Senior-level staff position:* makes sure that projects are on schedule and within budget; maintains editorial standards of the publisher	Salaried
Project editor	*Mid-level staff position:* moves manuscripts through the publication process; often responsible for hiring freelance assistance	Salaried
Editorial assistant	*Entry-level staff position:* provides office support and performs some beginning editorial tasks	Salaried

Minimum rates noted are for beginning but skilled editors working with low-budget clients. Rates vary widely depending on (a) the complexity of the job, (b) the expertise/skill of the freelancer, (c) the ability of the client to pay, and (d) additional demands, such as rush or technical skill requirements. For more details, see appendix B, "Editorial Skills, Rates, and Paces."

Proofreaders

Many people begin an editorial career as a proofreader. Proofreaders check a manuscript in its final form at the end of the production cycle. They catch errors that editors have missed, including faulty punctuation, spelling, numbering and listing, and type formatting. They also check word breaks, spacing, and sometimes page layout. Proofreaders might read final pages against another document for accuracy, or they might read pages *cold,* without comparing them to anything.

The best proofreaders

- have an excellent command of English grammar, spelling, usage, etc.
- understand style and work with style manuals and style sheets
- pay close attention to detail
- understand formatting and design issues: fonts, layout, etc.
- communicate clearly and tactfully with authors and other editors

Proofreading is sometimes combined with other editorial functions, but publications with the highest standards hire someone at the very end of the process to read with fresh eyes and to focus exclusively on proofreading. Although editorial assistants sometimes perform this function for book publishers, freelancers more commonly do so. Magazines and corporations might have staff proofreaders or might hire freelancers.

The proofreader comes last in the editorial process and is considered part of production. I have described this role first, however, because editors often begin a career by offering this service. Because proofreading is less subjective than other editorial tasks, clients are sometimes more willing to hire someone without a proven history to take this responsibility. A good proofreader early in a career will pay sharp attention to the work that editors have done on earlier stages of a manuscript and will learn from the work of those editors. A proofreader who earns the client's trust and proves ability might later be offered other types of editorial work. Some freelancers specialize in proofreading throughout a career, however, sometimes because they prefer the more objective role and sometimes because they enjoy working with design and typography, which are not of concern to many editors.

Proofreaders tend to earn the least pay per hour of all editorial freelancers, with some nonprofits, independent authors, and publishers paying the lowest rates. Corporations often pay considerably more.

Copyeditors

If you envision an editor as someone who examines every letter and punctuation mark on a page, you might be thinking of a copyeditor. Copyeditors scrutinize every sentence in a manuscript to ensure correctness and consistency. This includes checking and correcting spelling, punctuation, capitalization, and hyphenation. Copyeditors labor over every word, every comma, every *100* or *one hundred*. Levels of copyedit vary depending on the needs of a manuscript and on the publishing schedule and budget, but copyeditors always correct errors (in grammar, spelling, usage, etc.), ensure consistency (in capitalization, hyphenation, number treatment, etc.), check sequencing, query authors as needed (ask questions to clarify), and flag inappropriate use of language. Copyeditors sometimes also check artwork and references, smooth awkward phrasing, ensure logic, code copy for composition, and more. See "Levels of Copyediting" for tasks usually associated with different levels of copyediting.

The best copyeditors

- have an excellent command of English grammar, spelling, usage, etc.
- have a good ear for language
- understand style and work with style manuals and style sheets
- pay close attention to detail
- are able to create a style sheet
- respect the author's voice and style
- communicate clearly and tactfully with authors and other editors

Most book publishers hire freelance copyeditors. Magazines and corporations might use staff or freelance copyeditors or both. Particularly outside of traditional publishing (books and magazines), clients often combine copyediting with other functions—sometimes developmental work, sometimes proofreading, sometimes both. Good freelancers ask questions if the client's expectations are not clear.

Copyeditors typically earn more than proofreaders earn—but not always. They generally earn less than developmental editors do. Most start on the low end of the scale, with those who work at heavier levels earning more. Corporations typically pay more for all levels of copyediting than publishers do.

Levels of Copyediting

Every copyeditor must

- follow the instructions of the publisher, client, or other employer

- prepare a style sheet for use by anyone working with the manuscript

- *tactfully* query the author regarding inconsistencies, missing information, and apparent errors

- make corrections using a software program determined by the client, or mark the manuscript neatly and clearly using standard marks

Tasks will vary, depending on the level of copyedit. Each level requires the tasks included under its own heading as well as all tasks under lower-level headings.

A light-level copyeditor

corrects errors in

- grammar
- spelling
- punctuation
- usage

ensures consistency and adherence to house style regarding

- spelling
- hyphenation
- capitalization
- punctuation
- number treatment
- quotations
- abbreviations and acronyms
- headings
- lists
- fonts (italic, bold, etc.)
- usage

checks sequencing of

- numbered and lettered items
- alphabetical order

calls attention to or gets rid of

- biased language
- stereotypes

checks cross-references

checks contents against manuscript

A medium-level copyeditor also

corrects and/or notes stylistic problems, such as

- inconsistent or troublesome tone
- clichés, jargon, and mixed metaphors
- overuse of passive or impersonal constructions
- overuse of parentheses, italics, or other typographical devices
- lack of parallel structure in headings and text
- detours, dead ends, and repetition
- wordiness

checks for internal consistency in

- chronology
- percentages
- logic

calls attention to

- passages that might be libelous
- passages that might be plagiarized

A heavy-level copyeditor (sometimes called a substantive editor) also

corrects stylistic problems, such as

- wordiness and triteness
- sentences or paragraphs that are too short or too long
- repetition of pet words and phrases

makes sure that the manuscript is organized as far as

- the order of ideas presented

- the development and presentation of evidence

- paragraphs and transitions

- levels of heads

- relative length of major and minor points

Depending on the specific manuscript, the copyeditor might be asked at any level to do other things, such as

make sure that the manuscript parts correlate, particularly regarding

- text and objectives, summaries, review questions, and/or glossaries

- bibliography and text citations and/or footnotes

- numbering of pages, footnotes, tables, and/or illustrations

- callouts (cross-references, art placement, and/or footnotes)

check artwork (tables, maps, charts, illustrations) to make sure that

- it makes sense and is correct according to the text

- like pieces are treated consistently

- labels and captions match the style of the text (re spelling, hyphenation, capitalization, etc.)

edit documentation (footnotes, bibliographies)
format, add styles, or code files
note text, tables, or illustrations that might require permissions

Sometimes the copyeditor is also responsible for cleaning up the manuscript: incorporating the author's replies to queries in a later pass.

Editorial Proofreaders

Although separate copyediting and proofreading passes ensure the cleanest possible publication, some clients ask one person to perform both functions on a manuscript simultaneously. When this happens, the client sometimes labels the job proofreading, sometimes copyediting, and occasionally editorial proofreading. Editorial proofreaders might enter the publishing process when a project is on a tight deadline (with little time available for copyediting and proofreading), when a manuscript has been heavily copyedited or reformatted (and additional errors are expected in later versions), or when previously published material is to be reprinted (and does not require a full copyedit).

Editorial proofreaders have skills required for both proofreading and copyediting. The best editorial proofreaders

- have an excellent command of English grammar, spelling, usage, etc.
- have a good ear for language
- understand style and work with style manuals and style sheets
- pay close attention to detail
- are able to create a style sheet
- respect the author's voice and style
- understand formatting and design issues: fonts, layout, etc.
- communicate clearly and tactfully with authors and other editors

Many nontraditional publishers—such as corporate publications departments—rely on editorial proofreaders to perform the duties of both copyeditors and proofreaders. Corporations might have editorial proofreaders on staff, often with the job title of copyeditor, proofreader, or editor, or they might have a publications manager handle this task.

Editorial proofreaders should be paid on a scale similar to that of copyeditors or more.

Substantive Editors

Sometimes referred to as *line editors*, substantive editors complete all of the tasks listed under the higest level of copyediting (see "Levels of Copyediting," pages 23–26). In addition, they work heavily with sentence structure and wording. They smooth transitions, work on headings to improve logical structure, and sometimes suggest additions to or deletions of text. Substantive editors improve the flow of text and sometimes rewrite for consistency of tone or to improve focus.

The best substantive editors

- have an excellent command of English grammar, spelling, usage, etc.
- have a good ear for language
- are able to recognize an author's intent
- are able to work with the English language to improve clarity and flow
- are able to maintain the author's voice when appropriate
- are able to create a consistent voice among multiple authors when appropriate
- are able to reword succinctly
- understand style and work with style manuals and style sheets
- pay close attention to detail
- are able to create a style sheet
- communicate clearly and tactfully with authors and other editors

Substantive editors sometimes work on staff, sometimes as freelancers. Often they work with corporate publications, where the voice of the author does not need to be maintained. Sometimes they work with publications that have multiple authors and that need to be written in one voice. Nonnative-speaking scholars also sometimes hire substantive editors to help them polish dissertations written in English as a second language.

Substantive editors typically get paid more than copyeditors.

Developmental Editors

Whereas copyeditors pay attention to the nitty-gritty details of every word and sentence, developmental editors, or DEs, view the manuscript through a wider lens. They work with authors through the phases of writing and revision to ensure that manuscripts reach their potential. Developmental editors address broad issues of content and organization, always with the goal and audience of a manuscript in mind. Developmental editors identify gaps in content, delete divergent content, rewrite and restructure text, work with art, and sometimes coach writers throughout the process of writing a book.

The best developmental editors

- have strong analytical ability
- have strong organizational skills
- are able to empathize with authors
- are able to evaluate the objectives of a publication
- are able to envision a project and structure that best meet the author's goals and the reader's needs
- are able to work with the English language to improve clarity and flow
- are able to work with art and other visual elements
- have an excellent command of English grammar, spelling, usage, etc.
- have a good ear for language
- understand style and work with style manuals and style sheets
- communicate clearly and tactfully with authors

Because DEs are involved with content development, subject matter expertise can benefit these freelancers. Some publishers in some subject areas, in fact, require subject matter expertise for developmental editors. This is often true, for example, for editors working with medical material or with curriculum development. For developmental editing, publication as an author can also be helpful, because good authors often understand the process of organizing a book.

Developmental editors often find work with educational publishers. Editors who learn this skill might find other freelance work as well. Increasingly, authors who want to self-publish also hire DEs to help them create their manuscript. Book projects for freelancers include both nonfiction and fiction.

Getting It Right

Editorial focus varies depending on the task requested. A good copyeditor needs to notice every semicolon, every number, every slightly inaccurate word choice. But an editor who can't read past a misplaced comma or skip over a ten-letter word without looking it up might have difficulty getting the broad view required for developmental work.

Pay for DEs is generally higher than for copyeditors, comparable to that of substantive editors or a bit higher. Developmental editors who coach writers directly or serve as consultants throughout the publishing process often make even more, sometimes considerably more, especially with experience.

Technical Editors

In a narrow sense, technical editors work on computer-related publications—anything from programmers' guides to user guides or marketing materials, in both print and digital formats. In a broad sense, technical editors work with any type of difficult or scientific material, also including medical publications, environmental reports, financial documents, engineering manuals, and so on. The Society for Technical Communication broadens the definition of technical editing even more to include the following:[1]

- Communicating *about technical or specialized topics,* such as computer applications, medical procedures, or environmental regulations.
- Communicating *by using technology,* such as web pages, help files, or social media sites.
- Providing *instructions about how to do something,* regardless of how technical the task is or even if technology is used to create or distribute that communication.

Technical editors ensure that difficult information is presented clearly so that readers can understand it. They work with documents in both early and late stages, suggesting ways to improve layout as well as content. Their job might involve working with information design, identifying gaps in content (and providing more information if needed), deleting inappropriate content, rewriting and restructuring, checking math in text and tables, and performing other copyediting and developmental editing tasks.

Technical editors do not always need to have a thorough understanding of the subject matter they work with, but they must be able to find inconsistencies, holes in logic, and so on.

---

1   Society for Technical Communication, "Defining Technical Communication," www.stc.org/about-stc/the-profession-all-about-technical-communication/defining-tc, accessed February 3, 2013.

The best technical editors

- have an excellent command of English grammar, spelling, usage, etc.
- are able to evaluate the objectives of a document
- are able to diagnose the needs of an audience
- are able to structure a document to meet the objectives of the author and the needs of the audience
- understand technical material well enough to make it clear, simple, and readable
- recognize gaps in logic
- know when to look something up and how to find it
- are able to communicate with engineers and other subject matter experts
- understand style and work with style manuals and style sheets
- are able to create a style sheet
- are able to work with the English language to improve clarity and flow
- have excellent proofreading and copyediting skills
- communicate clearly and tactfully with authors

Technical editors might work on staff or as freelancers. They work for software companies, medical facilities, engineering companies, journals, financial institutes, government and university publications, and independent clients.

Technical editors are often the best-paid editors in the industry, whether the work is more difficult or not. Some technical editors also work for book publishers, and those might make the high end of the publishing pay scale but significantly less than their colleagues working directly for big business. Rates depend on the subject matter and the client.

Fiction Editors

Fiction editors might be asked to coach an author, work on development, or copyedit. Book publishers are most likely to hire freelancers only to copyedit or proofread because they rarely sign on a novel that still needs development, and when they do, staff editors work directly with authors. Independent authors seek editorial assistance for fiction at all levels.

Freelancers who hope to work with fiction must have all of the skills for the particular type of edit needed and must also be extra sensitive to the voice and style of the author. Especially if working for a publisher, the fiction editor should minimize edits, sometimes accepting odd spellings, aberrations in punctuation, and so on, as long as they are consistent and make sense. Beginning authors sometimes ask for more help with writing, and freelance editors with a strong background in fiction might get particular satisfaction from working with these clients.

The best fiction editors

- empathize with authors
- respect the author's voice and style
- are particularly attentive to logic and sequence
- have an excellent command of English grammar, spelling, usage, etc.
- have a good ear for language
- understand style and work with style manuals and style sheets
- are able to create a style sheet
- have excellent proofreading and copyediting skills
- communicate clearly and tactfully with authors

Independent authors who are self-publishing sometimes want to work with fiction editors who have published original fiction and can advise them throughout the process.

Book publishers pay fiction editors rates similar to nonfiction rates. Independent authors pay more or less, depending on their needs and on their ability to pay.

Web Editors

Web editing can be a variation of copyediting, developmental editing, or anything in between. In addition to having the skills listed for copyeditors and/or developmental editors, web editors should understand how readers process what they read on websites. Web editing requires tightening content and getting a lot of material into a few words.

The best web editors

- understand how readers process written material on the web
- have an excellent command of English grammar, spelling, usage, etc.
- have a good ear for language
- understand style and work with style manuals and style sheets
- are able to create a style sheet
- are able to condense a large amount of material

- are able to reword succinctly
- are able to work with the English language to improve clarity and flow
- have excellent proofreading and copyediting skills
- communicate clearly and tactfully with authors and other editors

An understanding of search engine optimization (SEO) is also helpful for web editing and is sometimes required.

Pay is typically on the higher end of the editorial scale for copyeditors and even higher for substantive or developmental editors.

Indexers

Some freelancers specialize in indexing, whereas others develop indexing skills in addition to other types of editorial skills. Indexers create an alphabetical list of concepts within a text to help a reader navigate a publication. Traditional book indexers are trained to organize entries in a manner that is most logical for readers to use. Good indexers work not only with words, such as names, but also with ideas, not searchable by computer but requiring thought and logic. They often work with a special software product, such as Macrex, Cindex, Sky, or (for web indexing) HTML Indexer. Indexing occurs at the end of the production cycle, after the book is set in pages, just before it goes to press. When other tasks in the publishing process have fallen behind, the indexer's schedule sometimes gets crunched, so indexers especially need to be able to work quickly under pressure.

The best indexers

- have an excellent command of English grammar, spelling, usage, etc.
- pay close attention to detail
- have strong analytical skills
- are able to conceptualize ideas
- have strong organizational skills
- understand style and work with style manuals and style sheets
- have excellent proofreading and copyediting skills
- communicate clearly and tactfully with authors and other editors
- are able to work accurately under pressure

Publishers sometimes hire freelancers directly to create book indexes. Increasingly, though, publishers are requiring authors to provide their own indexes. While some authors create the best index they can, others hire a professional to produce a professional-quality index.

Indexers often charge by the page or by the entry rather than by the hour. Rates vary depending on the difficulty of the material and the type of index required. Indexers charge considerably more for difficult or technical material than for other work.

Production Editors

Freelance production editors manage publishing projects from manuscript to delivery of bound books. They develop schedules, select people to do the work, see that each part of a job is done correctly, coordinate interdependent aspects of a job, get materials to and from the right people, monitor costs, and keep projects on schedule.

The best production editors

- have excellent managerial skills
- understand budgets
- have excellent time management skills
- have excellent command of English grammar, spelling, usage, etc.
- understand style and work with style manuals and style sheets
- understand formatting and design issues: font, layout, etc.
- have excellent proofreading and copyediting skills
- communicate clearly and tactfully with authors and other editors

Most publishers hire production editors, or project editors, on staff. Some hire freelancers to handle specific projects, however. Employees with other types of organizations often handle this responsibility themselves but occasionally hire freelancers to assist.

The tasks asked of a freelance production editor vary from overseeing a project to providing hands-on editorial services. Pay, too, varies depending on the demands of the job.

Keep in Mind

Do what you do well; don't try to do everything.

Staff Editors

Because this book is intended for home-based editors, the following descriptions for staff positions are brief. Anyone who works in publishing will benefit from a basic understanding of all editorial functions, however. Furthermore, because these staff members often hire home-based editors, it's especially important to understand what they do at the publishing house.

Acquisitions editors find the books and authors that a company will publish. They analyze the market, find publishable material to meet the needs of a given market, locate authors, and/or communicate with the editorial team regarding marketing goals of a project. Acquisitions editors sometimes rise through marketing channels. This senior-level position is typically reserved for a staff person.

Managing editors generally work on staff. They plan for publishing and make sure that projects are on schedule and within budget. These senior-level editors are responsible for maintaining the editorial standards of the publisher. The position combines many of the talents and qualifications of other types of editors.

Project editors traffic manuscripts from acquisitions or developmental editors within the publishing house. As publishing staff, they carry out the functions of the production editor, described earlier in this chapter. Project editors are often responsible for hiring freelancers.

Editorial assistants perform a variety of administrative and entry-level editorial tasks. These publishing novices might start mostly with word processing and filing, but capable and ambitious editorial assistants soon help with other tasks, such as proofreading, working with authors, and/or writing marketing copy. Many people launch a publishing career through this entry-level in-house position.

For Whom Will You Do It?

In addition to considering what skills you might offer, think about where you might want to work—whether for traditional publishers, for other kinds of businesses, or for independent authors. For a summary of the different types of clients, see "Potential Clients for Editorial Services." For more detailed descriptions, read on.

Business	Freelance Services Commonly Requested	Typical Pay
Book publishers	Proofreading, all levels of editing, indexing	Relatively low
Magazines	Proofreading, copyediting	Relatively low
Trade journals	Proofreading, all levels of editing	Varies
Scholarly journals	Proofreading, all levels of editing	Relatively low
Corporate publications	All levels of editing	High
Technical publications	All levels of editing	High
Institutional publications	Proofreading, all levels of editing, indexing	Relatively high
Advertising and design agencies	Proofreading, copyediting	Relatively high
Independent authors	All skills	Varies widely

Book Publishers

Book publishers, large and small, typically hire home-based editors to provide proofreading, copyediting, and sometimes indexing services. Publishers sometimes hire developmental editors, production editors, or other freelancers as well. Book publishers can be further divided into the following categories:

■ **Trade publishers.** These publishers produce books for the general population—the sort of book you might find in a bookstore chain. Some trade publishers add only a few books to their list each year, whereas others publish hundreds of books annually. Some have narrow interests, whereas others handle a much broader range of subjects.

■ **Educational publishers.** Some publishers target el-hi students with books for elementary and high school programs, whereas others produce textbooks for college students. Again, subject matter can be narrow or broad. Some educational publishers look for editors with experience developing curriculum.

- **University presses.** Many universities have affiliated presses that publish scholarly and other writing. University of Chicago Press, publisher of the esteemed *Chicago Manual of Style,* is one such well-known press. Some university presses look for editors with advanced degrees and/or foreign-language skills. Working for this type of publisher is viewed as prestigious, and editors often find the work to be especially satisfying.

- **Professional publishers.** Some publishers focus on books for one or more professions, such as business, education, or psychology. For editors with a special interest or area of expertise, these can be good targets for work.

- **Specialty publishers.** Quilting? Astronomy? Chinese literature? Publishers specialize in all sorts of interesting topics. Often these publishers are small, with small print lists, but for editors with a particular background, they can be a good source of work.

- **Packagers and production services.** Publishers sometimes contract with packagers and production services to produce books that are then published under the publisher's name. Although not publishers, these services often hire freelancers in turn to help produce the books.

Many editors focus on finding work with publishing companies; publishers understand good writing and provide rewarding work. The downside to working for publishers is that they tend to pay on the low end of the scale, sometimes a fraction of what tech companies or other corporations pay. Ironically, some of the most prestigious and difficult books—university publications, for example—can bring the lowest pay rate. Even so, many editors choose to focus on books. Others balance work on the books that interest them with other work that pays better.

Magazines

Most magazines hire staff to edit and proofread their publications. Some, however, hire freelance copyeditors and/or proofreaders. If you land one of these jobs, you could have regular work with a theme that interests you. Other magazines hire freelancers to back up staff members who are on vacation or take a temporary leave.

Trade Journals

Orthodontists? Woodworkers? Chefs? Winemakers? Many professions have trade journals, and while staff members usually create the content, freelancers sometimes provide copyediting and proofreading services. Trade journals can be good clients for editors with specific areas of knowledge, and the work is often ongoing and sometimes on a relaxed schedule.

Scholarly Journals

Often published by university presses, scholarly journals also have content specific to a particular subject matter. Like trade journals, scholarly journals offer ongoing work for editors and proofreaders.

Corporate Publications

Businesses produce all types of publications, and many understand that a good editor can help their image. Such publications include newsletters (both internal and external), direct mail pieces, human resources materials, catalogs, websites, and annual reports. Corporations vary in how they balance staff and freelance editorial work, but many hire at least some freelance assistance, sometimes for occasional work, sometimes for ongoing or repeat work. Pay is typically higher than for book projects, with annual and executive reports at the top of the scale.

Lessons Learned

Too often beginning freelancers jump into what they know, filling their time without exploring options. "I wish I had known about corporate rates," says freelance editor Christopher Bernard. "I began by working on what I knew, which was books, not knowing that there was a need for what I did in the corporate world; once I turned to that work, my income, very low as it was, immediately doubled."

Technical Publications

Technical publications, like corporate publications, often require the services of freelancers as well as staff editors. These publications include reports, product documentation, programming materials, user manuals, training guides, white papers, customer support materials, and marketing materials for both print and the web.

The amount of technical expertise required to work on technical publications varies. For product documentation and programming materials, the editor typically needs some understanding of the content. For user manuals, a layperson often makes the best editor, because an editor who already understands the material might not see when information is unclear. For marketing materials, technical expertise required depends on the purpose and the target audience.

Institutional Publications

Ever wonder who publishes all that patient information at your health care facility? How about the Medicare information sent out in reams? Publications departments sometimes produce this material—but often with the help of home-based editors.

Health care materials make up only a small share of the publications put out by institutions. Universities also put out masses of paper and thousands of web pages—even without considering university press books and professors' articles. University departments produce reports, alumni publications, press releases, event programs, and course catalogs, all in need of seasonal or ongoing help with copyediting and proofreading. No matter how small or large the university in your area, you might find publications in need of your services.

Reports, human resource materials, websites, and citizen communications of all sorts at all levels of government also require editing, sometimes freelance. Obtaining this work can be difficult; the government sometimes requires multiple bids for projects and piles of paperwork just to get considered for the work. But freelancers who jump the hurdles sometimes land repeat work, sometimes with good pay.

Advertising and Design Agencies

Some editors start out with an interest in advertising or design work. Others shift there from other fields. These clients produce short, snappy pieces as well as larger marketing materials. Sometimes materials are sent to an editor's home office for quick turn-around, but often freelancers are required to leave their home base to work on-site for these agencies. Freelancers typically help when an agency is in a crunch, and work in this setting can be fast paced and sometimes stressful. In other situations, agency work can be steady. Often it is relatively well paid.

Independent Authors

Increasingly, independent authors hire home-based editors to work with them on their publications. Some of these authors plan to self-publish, whereas others hope to increase their likelihood of impressing an agent or publisher by presenting a polished manuscript. Some want only proofreading or light copyediting, whereas others want higher levels of edit as they develop their projects. Working with independent authors can be particularly satisfying—or particularly aggravating. See chapter 9, "Working with Clients," for more about the rewards and challenges of working with independent authors.

Other sources of work directly for authors include projects for professors and graduate students, especially nonnative speakers. For more on working with scholars, particularly with students, see chapter 10, "Sizing Up Legal and Ethical Issues."

Pay rates for individuals vary widely, including some of the lowest around and also some of the highest. Again see chapter 9 for more on this issue.

Establishing Your Goals

Think about which of the skills mentioned in the first part of this chapter you have already mastered. Which appeal to you? Which seem attainable to you? Where will you start, and where might you build? Also, what kinds of clients would you like to work with? When you assess what you have to offer and establish your ideal clientele, you can begin to set goals for yourself and build strategies for developing your business.

03

Setting Up Your Home Office

What's Essential Now? What Can Wait?

Mary waves good-bye to her children as her husband, Marcus, scurries them off to school on his way to work. She pours herself a cup of coffee and retreats to the spare bedroom in the back of the house, where she has a comfortable desk with computer setup, a standing lamp, and two book-shelves, one for projects she has completed and the other for resources. She checks the messages on her voice mail and in her e-mail box, opens a manuscript in one window on her desktop screen and her working style sheet in another, and notes in a log the project title, the date, and the start time. Her workday has begun.

Adam seats himself at a desk in one corner of his apartment living room. In a hutch on one back corner of the desk are a dictionary and a copy of Chicago Style. *It's late afternoon, and Adam has completed his day's work as a part-time intern for a local magazine; he's eager to start on the disser-tation he has been proofreading for a grad student at the local university. Adam flips open his laptop computer, opens the dissertation, and begins work. An hour later, his partner, James, rushes past and disappears into a back bedroom. James knows this is work time. End-of-day chitchat will have to wait.*

Like Mary and Adam, 9.5 percent of the US workforce worked at least part-time from home in 2010, according to the Survey of Income and Program Participation.[1] This included 4.2 million self-employed individuals who worked

---

1 Peter J. Mateyka, Melanie A. Rapino, and Liana Christin Landivar, *Home-Based Workers in the United States: 2010*, www.census.gov/prod/2012pubs/p70-132.pdf.

exclusively from home and another 1.1 million who worked from home some of the time. Most freelance editors, in fact, work from a home base—whether a room designated specifically for the office or a table in a quiet corner with a computer on top and a bookshelf nearby. Some go to another location at times to work on the site of a client, but even those roaming freelancers typically have a base office at home where they handle marketing and administrative tasks and work on manuscripts for clients who do not require their presence. This chapter focuses on the home-based office as a physical space within the editor's residential structure.

Deciding on an Office in Your Home

Why choose to have an office at home? Working under the same roof with your bedroom and kitchen offers logistical advantages beyond the joy of being self-employed.

Save Time

When I commute from my home to an office in Berkeley twenty-two miles away, if I can adjust my start and end times to miss the commute rush, and if I can avoid accidents or other events that jam the roads, I make the trip in forty minutes. If I travel at prime time along with the millions of other Northern California commuters, that time can double. If an accident of any size has occurred on the highway, the time increases again. Multiply that time by two trips for start and end of day, then by five days in my workweek, and I easily face ten hours of unpaid work in a single week. That's more than a full day of work—or a full day of time off if I work at home. Walk down the hall to the office in my house, and my weekly commute drops to about five minutes.

Save Money

All of those miles from my home to Berkeley put wear on my car. At twenty-two miles each way, forty-four miles round-trip, even my hybrid drinks nearly a gallon of gas a day. The price of gasoline fluctuates, but the federal government in 2012 estimated that each mile driven cost a commuter 55.5 cents. At that rate, my 220 miles of commuting in a week would cost roughly $122—or more than $6,000 a year with a couple of weeks off. Granted, many people have shorter commutes. But many have longer ones—and/or the addition of bridge toll or parking fees. The walk down the hall might put wear on my shoes—but I can go barefoot if I want!

Add to the cost of transportation a budget for work clothes and another for lunches and/or coffee, and the numbers add up. The savings from working at home would pay for quite a vacation to fill the weeks spared by my down-the-hall commute.

Gain the Peace of Proximity

For some home-based workers, the peace of being close to a dependent can be invaluable. A call from a school office worker about a child with stomach flu can be a problem for both the school and a parent in an office far away. Although a home-based editor needs to refrain from jumping at every child's call, a quick trip to bring a child home to the comfort of a bedroom is usually easy to manage.

Choosing the Right Place

When setting up a workspace in your home, you might choose a separate bedroom or a den reserved exclusively for your business, or a corner of another room, or a cubicle separated in the basement by a partition. When selecting a space, consider

- where you will be able to focus on your work when necessary without distractions;
- how much space you need for your equipment, files, and other office items; and
- what space you have available.

Be realistic. You might find it harder than you thought to keep the television turned off if it's in the same room with you. The rest of your family might find it impossible to resist talking if you are in the same room with them. Or you might not be able to avoid that afternoon siesta if your work desk is in the corner of your bedroom. You need not only to maintain privacy in your space but also to have it relatively free of distractions.

Whatever space you choose, keep in mind that you can write it off as a business expense only if you use it exclusively for your business. You cannot claim that your entire bedroom is a business office just because you have a computer and a few books in one corner. You can write off the space required for that computer desk and bookshelf if you use them only for work, however, even if no wall separates them from the rest of the room. We will discuss writing off a home office in more detail in chapter 6, "Keeping Records and Paying Taxes." For now, just make sure the boundaries are clear.

Setting Up Your Home Office

After you select the space for your office, stock it with the things you will need for work. Start with things you already have. To edit, you really need just a computer, some sort of surface on which to place that computer, a good chair, and a good style manual and good dictionary, either in print or online. Add other items as you can afford them; avoid going into debt. For anything new, keep your receipts. You will need them when it comes time to file your taxes. See "Start-Up Costs Worksheet" to determine your personal budget.

Assessing Start-Up Costs

Setting up as a home-based editor requires little investment. Use the "Start-Up Costs Worksheet" as a guide. You probably already have the things you need most: a computer and a good dictionary. You might get away without spending anything at all to start your business. Even if you have nothing to begin with, though, you can probably manage for around $600 if you shop wisely and purchase, for example, a refurbished computer and a used style manual (see Minimum column in the start-up worksheet). If you want to step things up a bit—invest in a slightly more powerful computer, for example—you might spend $1,000 to $1,500, especially if you purchase used furniture (see Budget column). And if you have the resources, you might get a state-of-the-art beginner's office, complete with a new computer and ergonomic chair, for around $3,000 (see Full Deal column). Customize your own budget by adding numbers to the last column, under "Personal." If the total is too high, see what you can cut.

The numbers in the worksheet are rough; you might find deals for less or upgrade for more. In addition, freelancers who offer services that require special software, such as Macrex for indexers, will need to add that expense to initial costs. Nonetheless, estimates here will give you some sense of what to expect.

Establishing the Environment

Examine your space to make sure it is comfortable. How is your lighting? Natural light is good, but make sure it doesn't cause glare on your computer screen. A well-placed lamp can brighten your workspace.

Do you have enough power outlets in convenient places for plugging in a computer and other equipment? Do you need a power strip? A surge protector? Is the temperature of your workspace comfortable—cool enough in the summer and

Item	Minimum $	Budget $	Full Deal $	Personal $
Desk	existing table	25	300	
Filing cabinet	0	0	100	
Wall file	20	20	0	
Bookcase	bookends	25	150	
Chair	existing chair	30	250	
Lamp	existing light	30	30	
Power strip with surge protector	30	30	30	
Wastebasket	0	0	10	
Desk clock	0	0	10	
Telephone	existing phone	40	80	
Computer hardware	200	600	1,200	
Office software:				
without e-mail program	120	120	0	
with e-mail program	0	0	170	
Computer antivirus	80	80	80	
Backup system:				
Flash drive	10	10	0	
External hard drive	0	0	80	
Printer/copier/scanner	70	200	500	
Style manual/dictionary	30	45	65	
Mail scale	0	0	20	
Office supplies *	50	50	50	
Business license	25	25	25	
Business cards	10	10	10	
Total	645	1,340	3,160	

* Budget for paper, pens, pencils, Post-its, etc.

warm enough in the winter? Remember: You could be spending many hours a day in your office, and you will need to stay focused on your work. Would a room heater help in the winter if you don't want to heat the entire house when others are gone? If you do not have central air, is your space located in a relatively cool part of the house? A well-placed fan might help, but will it blow the pages of a manuscript from your desk? This isn't just about comfort; it's about productivity.

Choosing the Furniture

You will need a place to put your computer and a place to store your books and manuscripts. What does your ideal office look like? For starters, it might include an oak desk with a hutch and a file cabinet, an ergonomic chair, and some tall, stylish bookshelves. But take a look at a local office supply store or one online, and the numbers add up: maybe $300 for that desk you wanted, another $100 for a filing cabinet, $150 for a nice bookcase, $250 for your chair—and you haven't even looked yet at the big-ticket item: the computer. Is this something you can afford, especially without a paycheck to count on? Until you start earning some income, what are your options?

You probably already have much of what you need in your personal belongings. If not, and if you don't have someone to help you finance, think about ways to keep your costs down. Check local garage sales or thrift stores, and watch on eBay and craigslist for office equipment. A decent desk might cost only $25 second-hand— and bookshelves and filing cabinets might be about the same. You might even find someone to sell you a respectable piece of furniture for a buck and the cost of carting it away. If you must have new furniture, watch for sales late in the summer, when retailers appeal to college students on low budgets. As you increase your business, you can upgrade, but start low-cost and avoid debt.

Keep in Mind

While shopping second-hand can help you avoid debt, don't skimp on the chair. You will be spending a lot of time sitting while you work, so make sure you have a chair that is adjustable and comfortable for you.

If you are tight on space, you could create your own desk and file system by placing a board over two-drawer file cabinets for legs and setting your computer on top. Put up a few shelves if not a full bookcase. Make sure you find yourself a good chair. Second-hand is OK for this, too, but if you need to purchase one, try it out to make sure it is comfortable before you take it home. Keep in mind the principles of ergonomics, and be creative. (See "Ergonomics and the Workstation.")

To complete your furnishings, place a wastebasket and a box for papers to be recycled, tack a bulletin board on a spare wall, and set a file tray and maybe an organizer on your desk. Add a few favorite pictures and a calendar if you want, and you're ready for business.

Ergonomics and the Workstation

As an editor, you will spend many hours sitting while you work. Without care, this extended period of time at the computer could lead to eyestrain, repetitive stress injuries, back or neck pain, and other conditions of working with your body in one place for too long. With proper lighting, careful organization of your workspace, and breaks for stretching and movement, however, you can minimize your risk for discomfort and ongoing health issues.

Ergonomics is the science of designing and arranging things so that people can use them safely and efficiently. The study of ergonomics is ongoing, and a search on the Internet can lead you to the latest advice for setting up your workspace. Among key recommendations for a workspace are the following:

- **Lighting:** Light should be adequate for seeing text on a computer screen but not so bright as to cause glare or discomfort. Try variations in placement of a lamp and level of illumination until you find a combination that is comfortable and does not cause glare, either direct or reflected. If you will be working at night, check your lighting after the sun has set as well as during daylight hours.

- **Chair:** A well-designed, properly adjusted chair will provide necessary support for your back, legs, buttocks, and arms. Your feet should rest flat on the floor or on a footrest. Get a chair that is adjustable, one that will allow you to position yourself comfortably when you work. Also look for a chair that has a five-legged base and is easy to move so you can shift your position throughout the workday, reducing stiffness and the potential for achiness. Be sure to try out any chair before you purchase it to make sure it is comfortable for you.

- **Computer screen:** Monitors should be placed at a comfortable distance for reading with your head and torso upright and with your back supported by your chair. This generally means directly in front of you and 20 to 40 inches from your eyes, with the top of the screen at or slightly below eye level. Place the monitor perpendicular to a window to avoid glare. Experiment to find the most comfortable position for you.

- **Keyboard:** Set your keyboard up so it will be directly in front of you and your wrists, arms, and shoulders will be comfortable. When you use a properly placed keyboard, your shoulders should be relaxed, your elbows close to your body, and your wrists straight and in line with your forearms. Try using a wrist or palm rest to increase comfort.

- **Document holder:** Some editors use a document holder for printed materials at the computer. In this case, you might want to place the documents directly in front of you and slightly beneath the monitor. Documents should be close to the monitor and at the same height and distance as the monitor. When the holder is placed properly, you will be able to work without strain to your head, neck, or shoulders.

One resource, the Occupational Safety and Health Administration (OSHA), under the US Department of Labor, publishes guidelines that will minimize risk of injury on the job. In addition to setting up your workstation properly, OSHA recommends, shift your posture and work position throughout the day and take a five-minute break from computer tasks every hour. "Look away, stretch, get up, or walk," OSHA advises. "These brief pauses provide time for muscles and tendons to recover."

If eyestrain is a concern to you, ask your optometrist whether you might benefit from glasses prescribed specifically for computer work.

For more comprehensive and updated recommendations, see US Department of Labor, Occupational Safety and Health Administration, "Computer Workstations," www.osha.gov/SLTC/etools/computerworkstations/index.html.

Stocking Up on Office Equipment

I know a proofreader who does not own a computer. One. Proofreader, that is. He's one of the best proofreaders I know, and some of his longtime loyal clients still hire him to work on paper. Despite his outstanding reputation, however, he rarely gets a new client. No matter how much some of us might cling to our paper, insist on our bookstores with bound books, and argue that nothing replaces the turning of paper pages, we have to admit: It's the age of computers. And even clients who still want work done on paper (usually at late stages, when the publication has been laid out in design) expect to communicate by e-mail.

Computer Options

If you have a computer that you use for your personal life, or one that you used as a student, you might start your business without further investment. A computer designated for your work alone is a good early purchase, however, especially if you are sharing a machine with others; it keeps your business separate and protected. You will also be able to write off a work-only machine as a business expense, whereas you cannot write off a computer used for other purposes as well. If your budget is particularly tight but you need a computer, look for a refurbished model, one that has been restored to like-new working condition. You can sometimes get relatively new and respectable models refurbished for a good price. Watch for ads or search online. Get a guarantee at least until you have set up the system and made sure all is well, and consider spending a few bucks for a computer pro to look it over and make sure it's set up properly for you.

If you need to purchase a computer, one of your first decisions will be whether to invest in a PC or a Mac. Although you will find a few differences between the two systems in keyboard and graphics, those differences are relatively minimal. For the most part, too, editors who use primarily Word work equally well with PC and Mac computers; files can often be transferred seamlessly from one user to another and back (as between client and freelancer). Those who work with design programs might prefer one system over the other depending on the software used by a favorite client, but again, compatibility issues are minimal. If you are used to one system and like it, you might want to stick with it. If you have a primary client who uses one system, that might also help you make the choice.

Another decision is whether to use a desktop or a laptop computer. Desktops usually perform better for equal cost and are easier to upgrade if you want to add to them later. Laptops have the advantage of portability, of course, and also typically require less space in an office. Many established editors have a powerful desktop with a large monitor for easier viewing and also a laptop that can travel when necessary. This dual computer system provides protection for the occasional malfunction as well; when you are working on deadline, you cannot afford a day down if you need to take your computer to the shop. Two computers might be a goal for later in your career, though—not essential in the beginning. To start, choose one or the other based on your personal practices and space.

No matter what computer you have, be sure to have a backup system. One option is to use an external hard drive to back up your system automatically and regularly. Alternatively, you can copy files regularly to a flash drive and store them away from your system. You will also want to install a good antivirus to protect yourself from viruses, spyware, and other malicious threats. PCs are particularly vulnerable to viruses, but even Macs are susceptible. With the file sharing you are sure to do as a home-based editor, you will want to protect your system with an antivirus before you do anything else.

For most editors, Microsoft Office (for PC or Mac) will provide you with all the software you need in the beginning. Many editors work exclusively with Word.

Lessons Learned

Most every home-based editor has at least one horror story about hours of work lost when a computer crashed. Whether the loss amounted to many chapters or a few paragraphs, losing work is devastating. An employee who lost the same amount of work might be frustrated but would still take home a paycheck at the end of the day. But a freelancer cannot charge a client for the time to redo the work; the loss wasn't the client's fault or responsibility. The time is simply gone, unpaid. The solution? Have a routine backup system. Save your computer work frequently, and back up often. No matter how careful you are, you will probably experience this trauma yourself at least once. Investment in a backup drive—a flash drive for the budget-conscious, an external hard drive with automatic back-up, or even a second computer—will pay for itself in saved time before you know it.

Unless you are on an extremely tight budget, you will probably want to invest in an e-mail management program as well, such as the one that comes packaged in the home and business version of Office. As add-ons, indexers might also need to purchase special software (Macrex, Cindex, Sky, or HTML Indexer); proofreaders will be more marketable if they learn to mark up PDFs using Acrobat; and editors might be more in demand if they can work with InDesign or another basic layout program.

Computer Peripherals

In addition to a computer, you will want a few other pieces of office equipment. You probably already have some of these items, and you can purchase others as your business grows. Look for big-ticket items on sale, and consider buying second-hand if your budget is tight.

While seeking out *inexpensive* items, though, don't be *cheap*. You don't need top-of-the-line business machines, but you probably don't want bottom-of-the-line, either: Cutting costs too low can bring later regret when you find yourself struggling with a malfunctioning machine under a pending deadline. When shopping, check reviews, and ask for an in-store demonstration if possible. If you purchase a machine second-hand, try to get at least a short-term guarantee.

You will need a printer, even if you do most of your editing on-screen; most editors print out manuscripts when they have time for a final read. I like a good laser printer myself, because lasers spit out high-quality black-and-white printouts quickly. Inkjet printers are another option; they are often cheaper up-front and can be a good purchase, especially if you think you will need color. But they produce a lower-quality print, and ongoing costs (for ink per page) are generally higher. Don't be fooled by the relatively low cost of inkjet cartridges; toner cartridges for lasers cost more up-front but last significantly longer, so operating costs for a laser are actually lower.

Inkjet printers are also generally (although not always) slower than lasers. I know editors who balk when asked to print out a manuscript, or ask a client to pick up the expense, but I consider printing costs a business expense. The faster and cheaper my printer is, therefore, the better my investment. A printer that produces thirty pages a minute can print a complete three-hundred-page manuscript in ten minutes, whereas a cheaper machine producing ten pages a minute (or less) will require triple the time. Although this might not seem like a huge difference, the minutes will drag when you are working on a deadline.

Another thing to consider when purchasing a printer is whether two-sided print-ing is an option. If you expect to print long manuscripts frequently, this option could save you considerably in paper. Two-sided printing is also better environmentally—and even if you haven't joined the green movement yourself, some of your clients might ask you to get on board. One major client recently required all service provid-ers to fill out a survey regarding green practices, presumably with the intention of giving hiring preference to those who scored well.

Scanning can be a function of a printer, or you can purchase a separate scanner. If you plan to purchase a stand-alone scanner, find out whether multipage docu-ments need to be placed one page at a time or can be fed as a stack—and whether the machine can scan two-sided documents without refeeding. A multipage feeder might save you enough time to be worth the extra expense. If you have a good scan-ner, you probably don't need a fax machine, either; most anything to be faxed could be scanned and sent by e-mail instead, and with a scanner, you do not need to worry about an extra or a shared phone line.

Many printers and scanners also serve as copiers. If your machine does not make copies, you might purchase a separate machine—but don't buy too hastily. How many copies do you really need to make? Can you instead visit a nearby copy center or business store? Not only will a separate copier add to your expense; it might be unnecessary clutter in your office. Low-cost copiers are available, but they tend to be slow and sometimes jam easily. If you have a scanner, you can scan and print out documents in small quantity and visit a local copy center with high-end machines for bigger jobs. If you find yourself frequently needing to make these visits, reassess then. You can always add a home copy machine later.

Communications Devices

In this age of cell phones, many young people and some older ones forego a landline altogether. If you have a home business, though, seriously consider having not only a landline but a landline designated specifically to your business. If you must choose, you might designate your landline to your business and keep personal communica-tions to your cell phone.

Regardless of the type of phone you use, make sure the message your clients hear when you do not answer is professional. No client wants to hear your children, your dogs, your favorite song, or a humorous quotation. Even those who find your message cute or profound the first time they hear it will quickly become annoyed if they make repeat calls. Also, make sure your answering system allows a client to leave a message if you are speaking with someone else. Although telephone use has decreased as business has migrated to e-mail and other digital communications systems, a client who calls will be frustrated by a busy signal. Clients want to know that they have reached the right person and that you will get the message and return the call promptly. Then they want to get back to their work. One who can't leave a message might call the next person on the list of freelancers rather than try you again.

If you do use your cell phone as your business line, make sure that you have good reception in your office; no one wants to conduct business through static. Again, make sure the message is professional. And if you use the same phone for personal and business calls, find a way to distinguish when a call is for work. If you don't do this, you might find yourself working day and night seven days a week.

Finally, every professional this century needs to have Internet access and appropriate e-mail etiquette. Many Internet service providers are available to choose from, including some free ones. We will discuss this more in chapter 8, "Using the Internet."

A Mail Station

As an editor in the early twenty-first century, you will probably do most of your business by e-mail. Even so, you might need to go the old paper-and-envelope route at times. An inexpensive postal scale in your home office can make things easy and save you time. Have a few envelopes handy as well, including some large ones and some overnight mailers. Don't clutter your space with every imaginable mailing product; just get a few basics, and you will learn in time what more you need for your specific clientele.

Building a Library

In appendix A, "Resources for Editors," you will find many suggestions for online resources you can use to help you with your work, both for marketing and for doing the business of editing. I can't imagine a day, though, when I would not benefit from the myriad paper resources available for editors. Even if your budget is limited, you will probably want to invest from the start in a good style guide appropriate for the type of work you do and in a good dictionary. Supplement with online resources for a while, but add to your paper library as you are able. For details about the books mentioned here and more, see appendix C, "An Editor's Library."

Style Guides

If you are a book editor, you must have a copy of the latest edition of *The Chicago Manual of Style*. Now in its sixteenth edition, this bible of book publishing first appeared in 1906. Every so often, the editors in Chicago draw on their own experience and on input from other publishing professionals to rethink and reissue the manual in a new edition. Yes, you can get an online subscription to *Chicago*, complete with an online search function. But there's nothing like the worn pages of a manual littered with sticky notes at key entries.

When I began as a freelancer, I was advised to read *Chicago*—page for page. I never regretted the time invested in following that advice, and later, as a copyediting instructor for both Editcetera and UC Berkeley Extension, I required my students to read chapters from the manual. In addition to serving as a reference for style and usage, *Chicago* provides an overview of the publishing process. Buy the book used if you can find it, but get the latest edition; changes from edition to edition are always significant. Keep *Chicago* on your shelf where you can find it at any time and look up things as needed or digest entire chapters.

Depending on the types of publications you work on, you might choose a different style manual in addition to or instead of *Chicago*. Are you in journalism? You'll want *The Associated Press Stylebook and Briefing on Media Law*. A medical editor? You'll need *American Medical Association Manual of Style*. Are you interested in scholarship? *MLA Style Manual and Guide to Scholarly Publishing* or *Publication Manual of the American Psychological Association* might be a good choice. In tech? Consider *Microsoft Manual of Style* or *The Yahoo! Style Guide: The Ultimate Sourcebook for Writing, Editing, and Creating Content for the Digital World*. Many other style manuals are available, depending on your clientele. Purchase them as needed, and build your library as you go.

Dictionaries

Yes, you can check spellings online. But a good editor will want to have an authoritative, respected dictionary for more thorough checking. Many book publishers default to the most recent edition of *Merriam-Webster's Collegiate*. Some instead use the latest edition of *American Heritage*.

Why is the choice of dictionary important? Dictionaries are not all equal. Even reputable dictionaries vary from one another in their guidance for spelling, hyphenation, and capitalization, as well as in definitions and usage notes. Furthermore, dictionary editors continuously study our evolving language and update their publications with modern words and usage as they see appropriate.

It is important that you use the same dictionary that your client uses and always the same dictionary throughout work on a given manuscript. If you already have one or more regular clients, find out what dictionary they prefer and purchase it (even if it's not one of the two just mentioned). If you can't make a decision based on current work, make your own choice. *American Heritage* tends to be prescriptive, enlisting the advice of a panel of language experts to define words. *Webster's* is descriptive, capturing the voices of the American people and defining words as they are used. You might choose one or the other based on your own philosophy of the language— or you might choose whichever costs less at your local bookstore. I personally own both, as well as several other dictionaries, and I purchase the new edition each time one comes out. I started, though, with the dictionary I used in college, which happened to be the same one my first client preferred. By the time I replaced it with a new edition nine years later, the cover was well worn and the pages were frayed.

One of my favorite books has always been *Webster's Third New International Dictionary*—the twenty-eight-hundred-page tome with 476,000 word entries. Although publishers default to current collegiate editions when possible, this old comprehensive reference rarely fails to satisfy my curiosity when I look for the spelling or meaning of an obscure word. I purchased the 1961 version for over a hundred bucks when I started my business decades ago. It was a huge investment for me then, but those were some of the best hundred bucks I ever spent. (Alternatively, you can get a monthly or annual subscription to this publication at www.merriam-webster.com.)

Other Paper Resources

Next on your list might be a usage dictionary. Usage dictionaries, like standard dictionaries, follow philosophies ranging from prescriptive (prescribed by language experts) to descriptive (describing common usage). Some of my favorites are Theodore Bernstein's *The Careful Writer: A Modern Guide to English Usage* (not so "modern" anymore but still one of the most clear and concise manuals I have found) and Bryan Garner's *Modern American Usage* (more recently published and comprehensive). Other editors prefer *Merriam-Webster's Dictionary of English Usage,* which follows the traditional Webster's prescriptive slant and cites the history of word usage extensively. A look in *Webster's* at an entry for the word *hopeful,* for example, will lead you to two full pages of small-print type on the subject. Usage dictionaries can be expensive, and while you might want to acquire several eventually, choose your first one carefully. Borrow some guides if you can and look up a handful of troublesome terms to find out which approach you prefer. Alternatively, spend a few afternoons browsing at a local library before you invest.

Although you can find answers to grammar questions easily online, some answers are more trustworthy than others; you are likely to find as much bad advice as good when browsing the Internet. And although the spell checker that comes with Word can call attention to some (but only some) spelling problems, the grammar checker is wrong so frequently that I recommend turning it off. You can find Internet resources that are dependable, but I also like to have a good grammar book in my home library. Appendix C includes some suggestions. Specialized dictionaries (medical, geographical, biographical, biological, etc.), foreign-language dictionaries, dictionaries of technical terms, and atlases are just a few of the other resources you might collect in paper, depending on your particular niche and clientele.

Don't rush out to fill your shelves immediately; start with what you have, add a style manual and a dictionary if you don't have them already, use the Internet while you are building, and then slowly develop your paper library as you develop your clientele. Your entire business is about the written word, though, so take advantage of what's out there to help you provide superior work.

What Is This about Sole Proprietors and Business Licenses?

Like many people, I began my home-based editorial business with little planning ahead; I left my staff job with a promise of occasional freelance work from my former employer, a copy of *Chicago Style* and advice to read it, and a short list of local publishers known to hire freelance help. I had a bottom-of-the-line computer in a spare room at home and a bookcase with a few books on it. It didn't occur to me in the beginning that clients might exist outside of traditional publishing or that I should find those clients and make sure they found me. Nor had I given any thought to the idea that I was actually starting a business. I just knew I wanted to do what I had been doing—only more of it, and from my home.

Early on, I realized that I would have a more professional presence if I had some official stationery and business cards, and for those business cards, I seemed to need something more than my name. I added *Editorial Services* after *Barbara Fuller* and put it in writing, and that's who I became. I didn't register that name, so it never was official. It didn't matter. As years went by, I kept *Editorial Services* on my stationery but went primarily by only my given name. It was good enough, and somehow I succeeded.

But I had the advantages of a husband with a job, a small savings, and at least some immediate work from my former employer. Fortunately, in all my spontaneity and impulsive forging ahead, I didn't seem to make any destructive mistakes that would lead to legal trouble or send word that I was not to be trusted through the publishing community. I did have an ability to edit, and I seem to have had some common sense that served me well. I was good with numbers and had some intuitive business sense—and a mother who was an accountant and was always just a phone call away. I also had some luck, which is important for anyone starting out in a home-based business. But with better planning, I might have relied less on luck, and I might have grown more quickly into the business I wanted to be. If I had planned better, I might have succeeded more quickly.

> **Lessons Learned**
>
> "Really understand your priority. Then you can build a business that satisfies what you care about most—that's the beauty of freelancing and how it contrasts with climbing the corporate ladder."—A San Francisco–Based Freelance Editor

Choosing a Business Structure

I was in 1990 and still am a sole proprietor. Most home-based editors are sole proprietors: They work alone, taking all responsibility for their business and banking their own profits. According to the US Small Business Administration, editors are not unusual. Most small businesses start as sole proprietorships, and most continue as such. Sole proprietor is the simplest business structure to begin and to operate and works well for many.

Occasionally home-based editors follow a different business model. Some work as partners, particularly those who go into business with a significant other in a related occupation. Rarely a freelance editor sets up a limited liability company (LLC), usually with longtime business affiliates or, again, with a significant other. Although the sole proprietor model is by far the most common among home-based editors, it's worth thinking about other possibilities and learning at least the basic distinctions among business types. For an overview of advantages and disadvantages for four common structures, see "Advantages and Disadvantages of Business Structures."

Sole Proprietorship

Any home-based editor who has not specifically registered as another type of business is by default a sole proprietor. You do not need to take any legal steps to become a sole proprietor; you simply are, and you can begin work as soon as you

Type of Business Structure	Advantages	Disadvantages
Sole proprietorship	■ Easy to set up and run ■ Owner control of business and profits ■ Little regulation ■ Earnings taxed as personal income	■ Owner personally liable ■ Loans difficult to obtain ■ Business terminated on death of owner
Partnership	■ Relatively easy to set up and run ■ Shared responsibility for business ■ Shared skills and profits ■ Increased access to funding ■ Limited regulation ■ Earnings taxed as personal income	■ Potential for conflict of authority ■ Shared liability, including liability for partner's actions ■ Possible complications with business structure when one partner leaves
Limited liability company	■ Limited personal liability ■ Less recordkeeping than for corporations ■ Earnings taxed as personal income	■ More expensive to set up and run than sole proprietorship or partnership ■ Close federal and state regulation
Corporation	■ Limited personal liability ■ Ownership transferable ■ *S corporation:* Earnings taxed as personal income	■ Expensive to set up and run ■ Close federal and state regulation ■ *C corporation:* Corporate earnings taxed ■ *S corporation:* Restrictions on ownership

have obtained a business license in your community and registered a fictitious name if you decide to use one. As sole proprietors, single business owners work for themselves, as themselves. They determine and manage their own business and are entitled to all profits. Sole proprietors can change their status to another type of business structure whenever they want to do the paperwork and file the fees if their situation changes, but few do. They are less regulated and generally pay lower taxes than incorporated businesses.

As a sole proprietor, you are not your own employee but simply your own boss, responsible for your own business. You make your own decisions and determine your own strategies for completing your work and meeting legal requirements. You can move your business at will—or end it at any time. The business lives as long as you live and work and will die when you die.

Sole proprietors pay income taxes to the federal government at the start of each year, recording business income and expenses on Schedule C ("Profit or Loss from Business") and filing the schedule with Form 1040 ("U.S. Individual Income Tax Return"). Sole proprietors also pay self-employment taxes (Social Security and Medicare taxes), but they do not pay corporate taxes. Those who operate under their own name may use their Social Security number for tax purposes, simplifying records. They do not need to get a fictitious name or a Federal Identification Number (FIN), although they may do so if they would like.

The biggest disadvantage to working as a sole proprietor is that your personal assets are unprotected; your personal life and your business life are legally the same. You are responsible for all financial obligations of your business, and if your business were to be sued, you could lose your personal property. In reality, however, editors have few liability concerns (and those who are worried could explore business insurance with an insurance agent). Sole proprietors also have more difficulty obtaining business loans—but with low start-up costs this is rarely a problem, either.

Partnership

A partnership exists between two or more people who are in business together but are not either a limited liability company or a corporation. Government regulations for a partnership are not as severe as for a corporation, and the partnership is easier to start and dissolve. A partnership might be advantageous for two or more people with complementary skills—for example, two editors who trust each other to share work or an editor and a designer who could work together on a project. Married couples who do complementary work might form partnerships. If you enter a partnership, however, you need to feel confident of your ability to work together with others sharing your business and to trust each other. Not only do you share legal and financial responsibility, but your partner's work will affect your reputation.

Just as for sole proprietors, partners are not employees of themselves, and they file Form 1040 when they submit their taxes each year. Taxes and bookkeeping can be more complicated for partners than for sole proprietors, however. Partners must file an annual information return with the IRS, for example, and must obtain and use a FIN.

Partnerships can be disadvantageous if partners disagree about how to run the business or if one partner's work does not meet the quality standards of another. Partners share both profits and liability, which can be an advantage but can also be a disadvantage. Finally, if one partner leaves the business or dies, the business ends as it is.

Although partners are not required to have a written agreement, having at least the basics in writing is a good idea. These basics include, for example, details about the nature of the business and its goals, what each partner will contribute, what legal and financial responsibility each partner holds, and how earnings will be managed; provisions for what to do if one person leaves or dies or a new partner wants to join; and procedures for mediation in case of disagreement.

Limited partnerships are those in which one or more partners invest in the business but have limited liability. This is a more complicated arrangement and should be considered only with the advice of a lawyer and/or accountant.

Limited Liability Company

Sole proprietors or partners who are concerned about liability might consider setting up as a limited liability company. In this structure, liability is limited to assets of the business, as in a corporation, but the tax structure is similar to that of the sole proprietorship or partnership.

The LLC is a relatively new business structure in the United States, first used in Wyoming in 1977, and regulations and tax rules still vary from state to state. Few home-based editors choose this structure, but if it interests you, consult an attorney or an accountant to learn more. To set up, you will need to file the articles of your organization with your state's secretary of state.

Corporation

Another way to limit your personal liability is to set up a corporation. Corporations are also in a better position to get financial support from lenders and have increased access to insurance. Establishing a corporation can be costly, however, and involves extensive paperwork. Few home-based editors or other small business owners consider the potential advantages to be worthwhile.

Two types of corporations offer similar advantages in liability protection. Both involve shareholders, regular meetings, and officers. For the C corporation, or *regular* corporation, taxes are paid on the business itself, at a corporate rate; for the S corporation, taxes are paid on a personal level. Ownership of S corporations is limited, however, and other complex tax variations apply.

Companies with many employees often find the advantages of incorporation worthwhile. Independent freelancers, however, should think hard before they begin a process that can be time-consuming and costly, with complex tax and legal requirements and high administrative fees. Unless you expect to grow into something big—perhaps a full publishing business—you probably want to forego the *Inc.* after your name. If you do believe this might be a good choice for you, consult a lawyer and work with that lawyer to make sure you meet all legal requirements.

Naming Your Business

As a home-based editor and a sole proprietor, you might use simply your own name for your business: *Barbara Fuller* has served me well. For a partnership, you might operate under the names of the partners: *Fuller and Fuller.* Doing business under your own name requires no paperwork or registration and serves the purpose of clear identification. Alternatively, both sole proprietors and partners can create and register a fictitious name. Limited liability companies and corporations must also register a fictitious name if they want to use something different than the legal name filed in their articles of organization or incorporation.

Choosing a Name

If you choose a fictitious name, try to come up with something catchy to draw attention and make you stand out for potential clients. Choose a name that is clever but not cute, descriptive but not cumbersome. Think about how it will look on letterhead and on a web page. Look through directories of businesses—the Yellow Pages or a directory of editorial services. Try, for example, the editorial services section of industry suppliers in *Literary Market Place.* (See "What's in a Name?") Don't copy a good name; do this exercise only to give yourself ideas.

When you choose your name, make sure

- it immediately identifies what you do
- it reflects honestly who you are
- it is easy to pronounce and spell
- it is memorable
- it is original

Try starting with your given name. Can you do something with it? A play on a name can be catchy. If not, try adding part of your name to a description: Fuller Editorial Services. Think about the image you want to portray. Do you want to appear to be bigger than you are? A potential client might respect East Bay Editorial more than Fuller Editorial, even if it is exactly the same thing. East Bay Publishing would be misleading if you didn't offer full publishing services, so that probably wouldn't work. Or maybe you want to retain your personal identification and keep your given name after all. Whatever you come up with, use the search engine of the US Patent and Trademark Office website (http://tess2.uspto.gov) to make sure the name is

What's in a Name?

These names of editorial businesses are among 321 listed in the Editorial Services section of *Literary Market Place* 2012 online (accessed October 4, 2012). Which catch your attention? Which let you know immediately what the service is? Which will you remember?

The Author's Friend	The Permissions Group Inc
Beta Indexing Services	Pictures & Words Editorial Services
BookCrafters	Proofed to Perfection Editing Services
EditAmerica	Straight Line Editorial Development
Editcetera	Words into Print
InfoWorks Development Group	Wordsworth Communication
Little Chicago Editorial Services	The Writer's Lifeline Inc
Metropolitan Editorial & Writing Service	Writeway Editing

original. If you copy someone else's trademarked name and are later asked to stop using it, you must comply. Also check to make sure that a URL has not been taken for the name you want to use.

Getting It Right

Editcetera, the organization I head as director, began in 1971 as a cooperative of freelance editors. One of our founders, Loralee Windsor, suggested the name *Editcetera,* and that name has served us well: Often clients comment on how memorable it is. *Editcetera* wouldn't have survived for this long if clients hadn't been happy with our service, but the first thing to do when offering services is to catch the client's attention—and a clever name can help. *Editcetera* is both clever and meaningful.

Unfortunately, *Editcetera* has seemed like a good name to others through the years as well—whether those others thought of it independently or heard it somewhere and tried to take it as their own. Because we have registered our name as a service mark with the US Patent and Trademark Office, however, those others have had to stop using our name when requested. Changing a name could be confusing to clients and costly if it means replacing stationery and other items with the name on them. But protection of a name is important. In one disturbing situation, we learned that a business using our name had been providing inferior work—and charging unethically high rates—and we were eager to end any potential mistaken affiliation. Fortunately, we had the legal standing to do so.

Registering Your Fictitious Name

If you intend to start a business as a sole proprietor or a partnership under a name other than your own, you must in most states register a fictitious business name using a fictitious business affidavit, or a DBA (doing business as) statement. Note *most*; not all states require this registration. Those that do typically require you to file documents at the county level, usually with the county's recorder of deeds, although some states require partnerships to file with the secretary of state. Some also require placing a fictitious name notice in a local newspaper as part of DBA registration. If you first find a newspaper to print your notice, find out if the paper also files the necessary paperwork with your county; some small newspapers keep DBA forms and will help you through the process. Cost for registration varies by location but is usually $10 to $100, and most (but not all) states require renewal every five years or so. Limited liability companies and corporations file fictitious names if necessary with the secretary of state; rules for filing vary among states.

Registering your DBA lets your state government know that you are doing business under a name other than your personal name. You will use your DBA on all government forms and applications for your business, including licenses and bank accounts. Registration also enables you to claim the right to your name within a given jurisdiction (usually within your county) and to prevent others from operating under that name. This claim on identity can be important to avoid confusion and protect your reputation. Registering your name alone does not, however, provide you with trademark protection or make you a corporation.

Keep in mind that you do not need to file a DBA form if you use only your own name for your sole proprietorship or partnership. Some states also permit the use of strictly descriptive words—such as *editorial services*—without filing; check your state if you are interested.

Obtaining a Business License

Even if your business is small in the beginning and your income low, you need to obtain a local license to do business in most cities or counties. This applies no matter what type of business you have: sole proprietorship or corporation, editing or selling real estate or styling hair. License requirements vary by location and by business, so don't look to a friend with different circumstances for advice; find out what's necessary for your business in your community. Start by inquiring with your local chamber of commerce, city or county clerk or revenue department, or other municipal headquarters. Once you find the appropriate office, go to the office to obtain a form or check the office website to see if you can download one.

To get a license, you will need to pay a fee based on the amount of business you expect to do or, after you begin, on work actually done. In most communities, the fee is minimal—often under $100, sometimes considerably under $100.

If you neglect to get a business license where you need one, in the worst-case scenario, your business could be shut down. More likely, your community will somehow become aware of your negligence and insist on your compliance. For example, a Schedule C sent with Form 1040 as submitted to your state tax board indicates that you are operating a business, and the state might notify your local community. Sooner or later, especially with sharing of records through the Internet now and with governments short on revenue, your local community will probably notify you of your oversight. Municipalities operate in many ways, but notices are likely to be friendly and personnel happy to help you get into compliance as soon as you make the effort. Even so, you will probably need to pay a penalty and/or interest if you have not obtained the appropriate license at the outset of your business.

After you register your business and pay your fees, you will receive a paper license that you can post proudly in your office space. In some areas, you will be required to post your license. Be sure to note the expiration date and renew the license at the appropriate time.

For more information on business licensing for your community, see the Business Licenses and Permits page of the Small Business Administration website (www .sba.gov/licenses-and-permits). From there, you can access local information for your state or community.

Complying with Zoning Regulations

As an editor, you could work an entire career without ever meeting a client at your home office. If you do expect to have clients come to you, however, you will need to check local zoning laws. For the most part, cities allow home-based businesses with few restrictions. The restrictions that do exist, if any, typically regard

- physical changes to the appearance of your home, such as signage;
- traffic and parking for clients; and/or
- external effects or nuisances, such as noise or the use of hazardous materials.

Occasionally districts require home-based businesses to have a separate door for business associates to enter and/or to have a parking space. None of this is likely to apply to you as an editor, but be aware of the possibilities. Your local planning office can tell you if you need to adhere to any special requirements. And if you do need to meet with a client and don't think your home office is a good place, you can always go to the client's workspace or meet somewhere over coffee.

Understanding Insurance

Although many self-employed editors work without business insurance, others make the investment to protect themselves. Furthermore, some clients require any freelancers working for them to have insurance. If you work from a home office, you might want to research at least the following. Your insurance agent can help you determine a reasonable policy for your situation.

General Liability Insurance

Liability insurance protects a freelancer against negligence. For example, an editor might miss a crucial deadline or make a severe mistake that is costly to the client. Most insurance agents can set freelancers up with liability insurance to protect their home business. For about $250 a year, you might get $2 million in coverage, for example. Although freelance editors rarely need this insurance (never in my experience), the fact that you have it might make you eligible to work with a respected client. If you land a job with just one client able to pay you $5 more per hour than other clients you have, you could pay for the entire policy in a week or two and at the same time protect yourself against unlikely but possible problems.

Home Office Insurance

If you have expensive computer equipment in your home office, homeowner's or renter's insurance is unlikely to cover it; many home policies cover only about $1,000 for such equipment, and you will need to pay a deductible before you receive any coverage at all. A floater to your policy to cover your computer and data could be a good investment. Ask your insurance agent about options.

Setting Up a Bank Account

Although it's possible to keep track of business income and expenses on paper using your personal account, a business-only checking account can make it easier for you to track and justify business expenses, and a business-only savings account can make it easier to set aside money for annual or quarterly expenses, such as estimated taxes (see chapter 6, "Keeping Records and Paying Taxes"). You might set up a separate account using your current bank, or you might look for a new financial center. Talk to other freelancers in your area to see if someone can recommend a bank that might be right for you. When shopping, consider the following:

- What kinds of small business accounts are available?
- Can you do your banking online?
- Will you get interest in your savings account, and can that be linked to a checking account?
- How easily can you find someone at the bank to answer your questions?

Even if you do not have a separate bank or checking account, consider getting a business-only credit card. Again, this will simplify accounting.

Writing a Business Plan

For many individuals starting a business, the business plan is an essential tool for obtaining financial support. Of literally hundreds of home-based editors I know, however, I can't name one who obtained a loan from an investor to start a business; we editors tend to start less formally, depending on savings or support from family members to help us in the beginning. Furthermore, as discussed in chapter 3, start-up costs are minimal, unlikely to require a loan.

Even if you never present a business plan to lenders or anyone else, though, the act of writing one will force you to think about your objectives and to set goals and strategies for attaining those goals. The more you think about your goals and expectations before you begin work, the more likely you are to build a satisfying business. And the more you think about how you might get to where you want to be, the more likely you will stay on track through your journey. You can search the Internet or check in books such as this one to find guidelines for writing a plan, but don't worry about making it too formal; for editors, the plan is basically for you. Scrawl it on a legal pad if you want, or type it in an open document.

Be honest with yourself. Let yourself dream a little—but be realistic. What do you want to do? What do you need to do? What can you realistically expect to do?

Address some basic questions in the beginning:

1. What editorial services are needed in your community?
2. What services will you provide?
3. Who are your potential clients?
4. How can you learn about other potential clients?
5. How will your clients learn about you?
6. How will you convince your clients to hire you?
7. What resources do you have?
8. Where will you get the money to start your business?
9. What are your short-term goals? Your long-term goals?

If you are reading this book start to finish, you might be able to answer some of these questions now. You might have no idea how to answer other questions—for example, how *will* your clients find out about you? That's OK. Start with notes, and add to them as you learn. By the time you close this book after finishing the last chapter, you will probably have ideas to fill in the blanks.

Think of your plan as a roadmap to get you from the beginning of the list of questions (what editorial services are needed?) to the end (what are your goals?). If you think about this carefully, your business plan will serve as a guide and keep you on track as you develop. As when you follow any map, you might need to adjust at times—you might hit a roadblock and need to take a detour—but with discipline, you will be able to get back on track. Or you might decide to change direction at some point and redefine your destination altogether. That's ok, too, as long as you don't wander aimlessly along the way.

You can design your plan as you like, but give attention to the following elements.

Table of Contents

Use this directory to find things later, when you've almost forgotten that a plan existed but suddenly find yourself frustrated with your business. Place the contents first in the document.

Executive Summary

Although the summary comes second in your plan, you might need to revise it or even draft it after you complete the rest of your plan. Start with a mission statement of four sentences or fewer. State briefly the primary services you will offer, the things

Sample Executive Summary for a Business Plan

Mission Statement: I will combine my experience as a nurse and my skill as an editor to provide editorial services to publishers and businesses with a focus on health care. I will first offer copyediting services, but within three years, I will work primarily as a substantive editor. Clients will include book publishers, journals, and health care facilities that publish reports.

Because I am making a transition to editorial work from an earlier career in nursing, I have firsthand knowledge of the health care business. To prepare for my editorial business, I have completed proofreading and copyediting workshops with Editcetera and an online workshop in substantive editing with UC Berkeley Extension. In addition, I have purchased and studied *The Chicago Manual of Style* and *American Medical Association Manual of Style,* and I have *Stedman's Medical Dictionary.*

    I plan to start by targeting three local publishers with health care and nutrition books on their lists: trade publishers Ten Speed Press and Ulysses Press and professional publisher New Harbinger Publications. I will start by asking for informational interviews with all three with a goal of learning what their companies look for and what they would like to see in a substantive editor. I will also ask these publishers if they administer tests for potential freelancers. In addition, I will research health care organizations in my region and inquire about freelance opportunities with them, targeting one potential new client each month if I have paid work and each week if I do not have paid work. Finally, I will join Bay Area Editors' Forum in San Francisco and attend at least four meetings a year to network with other editors.

    I have enough savings that I can live without income for up to six months, but I will need to make at least $1,000 a month after that. I hope to have at least three clients in my first year and three more in my second. By my third year in business, I plan to have repeat work from my favorite clients and to do mostly substantive editing. I need to have an annual income of $30,000 net by three years from now.

that make you different from other editors, your target audience, your marketing plan, and your objectives in terms of work and financial success. See "Sample Executive Summary for a Business Plan" for an example of an executive summary.

Industry Analysis

Define your potential clients. Do you want to target publishers? Who are the publishers in your area? If none are in your geographical area, who are the publishers producing books that interest you and that might benefit from your particular services? Or are you interested in working with independent authors? Scholars? Health care companies? Software developers? Don't list every possibility—just the clients you want. Refer to chapter 2, "Envisioning the Business," to make sure you haven't forgotten anyone important.

Business Overview

Describe your business and the role it will fill. Explain the services you will provide and how you think you will be successful based on your location, experience, and so on. What are your business objectives? What skills will you offer? What makes you particularly well qualified to do the work you want to do? What resources do you have to aid you? Do you plan to increase your skills? How? Return to chapter 2 to remind yourself of possible skills. Also see chapter 12, "Developing and Expanding Your Business," for ideas regarding long-term directions.

Marketing Plan

Where will you find your clients? How will you market your skills? Will you take out ads in directories? Build a website? Join editorial groups that will post your résumé or offer links to your website? Will you reach out to potential clients directly? Request informational interviews? How? How often? This section is important. See chapter 7, "Connecting with Clients," for suggestions.

The Competition

How many other editors offer the same service you offer? What unique skills can you offer? Are you fluent in another language? Do you have computer skills that are less common but are sometimes required?

Plan of Operations

What do you need to start your business? In chapter 3, we discussed setting up a home office. We also noted items that were essential from the start and other supplies and equipment that you might want to purchase as you are able. What is your plan for obtaining those less-essential items?

Goals

What are your short-term and long-term goals? Where do you hope to be in a year? In five years? Do you expect to be busy full-time? Part-time? How many hours do you hope to work in a week, and how much income do you anticipate?

Funding Needs

While this section is primary for many people starting a business, editors are not likely to obtain loans to get their business off the ground. You can skip this section if you want, or use it to outline your financial plans as a budgetary reminder and guideline for yourself.

> **Keep in Mind**
>
> If you are like most editors and write a business plan to set goals rather than to support a loan request, you can make it informal—as simple as a single page handwritten on a yellow legal pad. "A plan doesn't need to be fancy or long," says San Francisco–based editor Geneviève Duboscq. "It just has to have thought and realism behind it."

After you have written your plan, read it over. Copy your executive summary and pin it to a bulletin board or tape it to a wall where you can revisit it frequently to remind yourself where you wanted to go. Then put the rest of your plan somewhere easily accessible. Revisit your plan as you like. Use it as it helps you. Deviate as you need, but if you wander, make sure it's because you want to wander and not just because you have no plan.

05

Managing Finances

How Much Do You Charge, and How Do You Get Paid?

Editors are word people. It's that simple. Many of us don't find numbers particularly interesting even if we do understand them.

As editors running a home-based business, however, we must be concerned with money—and that means being concerned with numbers. This isn't hard math. It's reality. Even some of the most talented editors too often find themselves in trouble because they have failed to plan ahead. A solid client base and a high pay rate won't necessarily preclude an anxious wait at the mailbox (or frequent checking of e-mail for notice of a deposit) come time to pay bills.

To be successful, any freelancer needs to establish reasonable rates that will cover all expenses, including infrequent but high expenses such as tax and insurance payments, and invoice and collect payments in a timely manner. You do not need to be a mathematical wizard to manage your finances. You do need to plan wisely, however. This chapter gives some suggestions for making sure your numbers work out and your income flows to keep you in the black. It also gives details for providing job estimates so you can be sure that you and your client are on the same page when it comes to billing.

How Much Can You / Should You Charge?

One place to start in financial management is to look at your family budget to see how much you need to make. How much do you need to contribute to your family? Think about your various ongoing personal expenses (rent or mortgage, food, transportation, entertainment, utilities and communications,

fees, etc.) and your occasional personal expenses (tax and insurance payments,
home maintenance, vacation, etc.). Then add your ongoing business expenses (office
supplies, phone, Internet, etc.) and your occasional business expenses (professional
fees, license, etc.). Finally, remember to include expenses for health insurance or
other benefits that you will need to cover now that you are self-employed.

Financial needs vary significantly, but if you have never established a family
budget, use the "Expense Worksheet" to begin calculations. After you arrive at a
total, if you have another family member contributing, deduct that amount from
your total household needs to determine your target contribution. Don't worry
about doing this entire exercise now, but follow through when you have time and
are ready—and when you do it, add a little to your final number for a pad. For now,
for the purpose of this exercise, let's say that you have done the math and determined that you need to put $3,500 a month into your family budget from your
business, or $42,000 a year.

How do you get to $42,000 a year? Easy. If you work fifty-two weeks in a year, five days in a week, eight hours in a day, you have 2,080 hours in which to earn $42,000. Divide $42,000 by 2,080 hours, and you need to make just over $20 an hour to meet your budget. Twenty dollars an hour is a reasonable goal for even beginning editors, so you're looking at a comfortable living. To give a pad, plan to make $25 an hour, multiplied by those same 2,080 hours, and you have $52,000. You're rich! Paint your house, enjoy a night on the town, and treat the neighborhood to a party.

Right?

Expense Worksheet

Your budget is unique to your household and your circumstances. This worksheet is intended only as a starting point. Use the extra spaces in each category on this worksheet or create your own worksheet to track other potential expenses as appropriate. See chapter 6, "Keeping Records and Paying Taxes," for information about estimated taxes (listed under occasional business expenses).

Expenses	Average $ per Month	x 12 = $ per Year
Personal—Ongoing		
Rent/mortgage		
Food		
Transportation		
Entertainment		
Clothing		
Utilities		
Communications		
Memberships/fees		
Other		

Continued on next page

Expenses	Average $ per Month	x 12 = $ per Year
Personal—Occasional		
Property tax		
Home/renters' insurance		
Auto insurance/registration		
Home maintenance		
Vacation		
Other		
Business—Ongoing		
Office supplies (paper, ink, etc.)		
Phone service		
Internet service		
Other		
Business—Occasional		
Estimated income tax		

Expenses	Average $ per Month	x 12 = $ per Year
Books/resources		
Professional dues/fees		
License		
Other		
Benefits		
Health insurance		
Dental insurance		
Disability insurance		
Retirement contribution		
Other		
Total Budget		
− contribution from other household member(s)		
= Contribution goal		

Wrong. The biggest problem with this logic is that you won't actually bill for forty hours of work each week during the year—especially not in the beginning. Many home-based editors find that they can concentrate enough to do careful editing for only about six hours a day. Most also spend many hours each week marketing, talking to potential clients who never do provide paid work, handling administrative responsibilities, and self-educating through workshops or reading—all unpaid. Although some do handle forty hours of paid work in a week, and sometimes more if a deadline requires it, most are able to bill for only twenty-five to thirty hours a week on average. For the purposes of this exercise, let's say that you can actually bill for thirty hours a week. Thirty hours times fifty-two weeks at $25 an hour nets you $39,000. Now you're just shy of your $42,000 goal—maybe close enough to make it if you live frugally.

But we've accepted that you aren't going to get paid for forty hours a week even if you work forty hours a week. Are you really going to work fifty-two weeks a year? What if you get sick? Say you're reasonably healthy and need to stop work for only one week during the year. Or you're extremely healthy but your eight-year-old son is home one week, too sick to be in school but not sick enough to lie quietly while you work. Plan on at least one week of sick time. And what about Great Aunt Matilda's one hundredth birthday celebration across the country? You thought you could hide in a corner with your laptop, but your cousins are determined to hear about everything you've done for the past twenty years. That's two weeks without pay. Now you've lost another sixty hours, or $1,500 (two weeks x thirty hours x $25 an hour), and annual income has dropped to $37,500.

You don't mind working straight through Labor Day week—or working four long days to give yourself an extra day off. You're willing to work on Martin Luther King Jr. Day and on Veterans Day, even though your daughter home from school doesn't understand and keeps interrupting. But you must want *some* time to celebrate *something*—maybe an extra day off for Yom Kippur or Christmas. Conservatively, let's say that you give yourself two holidays during the year. Twelve hours off equals $300 in lost pay, bringing you down to $37,200.

So much for making $52,000 by billing $25 an hour. Even if you *can* keep a steady flow of work, is this enough? And even if you reduce your expectations for the family budget (maybe cut some clothing and dinners out), can you make ends meet? What started as a comfortable $52,000 has shrunk by nearly $15,000, far short of your original budget.

How can you adjust?

- Cut costs. But where? More from your family budget? Is that possible?
- Work more hours. This requires (1) that you have the time to work more and (2) that you convince enough clients to hire you. If you do get the extra work, can you keep your concentration during the extended hours? As a home-based editor, you can't afford to do inferior work when you are exhausted, so overworking might not be a good idea.
- Increase your rate. Are you underbilling for what you do? If not, can you increase the value of what you have to offer? How?

If you are short in meeting your budget, maybe you can raise your rates for what you already do. If not, think about ways to increase the value of what you offer. See chapter 12, "Developing and Expanding Your Business," for ideas. For now, let's look at what you can reasonably charge. Is $25 too little? Although many beginning editors consider this acceptable (or even good), long-term committed professionals often average more.

Setting Rates

No matter how much money you want to make or think you need to make, you must be realistic if you hope to get any work at all. Rates vary considerably among editors, based on

- type of service offered
- experience and skill level of the editor
- ability of the client to pay
- demands of the job

Type of Service Offered

Developmental and substantive editors generally earn more per hour than copyeditors do, and copyeditors earn more than proofreaders do. Ranges are broad, with specific numbers determined by other factors, but for a given project with a given client, task performed could be the first determinant of rate. See appendix B, "Editorial Skills, Rates, and Paces," for ranges of pay for various skills. If you are not able to make enough to meet your requirements, could you add to your skill set? This might take time, but set a goal, and start working.

Experience and Skill Level of the Editor

When I began work as a freelance editor, I concentrated hard and consulted my style manual and other resources frequently. Often I worked through a manuscript three or more times but billed for only the first two passes; I considered the last pass a part of my learning process (a review of my own work) and didn't want the client to think I was too slow to be hired again. I always gave my best effort on the work, and I must have done an adequate job, because my clients invariably hired me back. But years later, when I began teaching copyediting and looked over past jobs in my search for examples, I sometimes felt embarrassed to see the mistakes I had missed or made. I sometimes wondered why those clients did ask me back. Colleagues have told me they had similar concerns in retrospect about their early work.

We all learn, and we all improve with experience. No beginner is as good as the more experienced self of the future. Through the years, I mastered much of *Chicago Style* and lodged it in my memory, I got so I could make decisions without consulting a source at all, and I learned to correct things that seemed to be okay but really weren't. As my work improved, I also established processes that made me more efficient. Although every manuscript is different, I learned common things to look for and ways to communicate better with authors. Furthermore, as my work improved, the editors and proofreaders who followed me had fewer things to clean up and could therefore work faster and better.

Of course a client might pay more per hour for an experienced editor with a proven record. Editors newer to the business might need to accept a lower rate while building a reputation but should raise that rate as their skills improve. As you build

---

Lessons Learned

A student in a basic copyediting class I taught in the 1990s told me that he billed $45 an hour for his services. As his instructor and an experienced editor, I was surprised; he was still developing his skills, and $45 was high even for an experienced editor at the time. I wondered how he did it—until he told me a few weeks later that he had been able to get only one client since he started several months earlier, and that was a friend of a relative.

your experience, you will also be able to attract more of the higher-paying clients able to pay your higher rates.

Ability of the Client to Pay

Some clients have substantial net value. Some have less.

Scholarly publishers, for example, produce great books that often require great skill to edit, and editors who contribute to such masterpieces should take pride in their work. But no one gets rich from working on scholarly books, and that includes the copyeditor. Part of the payment is in prestige, which doesn't help pay the bills (but which does add to a freelancer's credibility when marketing future clients).

Now compare work on a scholarly book to work on a marketing blurb for a deep-pocket tech company. Some work for tech companies is difficult and requires a level of expertise worthy of reward in higher pay. But large corporations sometimes pay relatively high rates even for work that is less difficult. If marketing materials are important to the success of the company, and if everyone working at the company is taking home a large paycheck, the freelance editor might also expect relatively good compensation.

How great is the difference in pay? A tech editor can make three times what a book editor makes in an hour. A proofreader of ad copy can make double the hourly rate of a proofreader for scholarly books. So choose your clientele. If you edit because you love to contribute to the publication of great books, stick to books. Satisfaction is worth a lot. But if you're unable to balance your own books, explore options for working with other kinds of clients. Consider having a mix of clients, some to provide you with the work you love most and others to give you the work that pays best.

Demands of the Job

Do you work in InDesign? A client in need of someone with that particular skill might be willing to pay extra for it. Does the client expect you to complete a forty-hour job in three days? If you are willing and able to put in the hours, you might get a premium. Does your client need you on call, able to take small jobs on short notice and turn them around quickly? Or do you have a reputation as someone who can work well with demanding and temperamental authors? These are all situations that might merit a premium. If you add extra value in terms of professional skills or work habits, you might find yourself in demand and be able to raise your rates.

Providing Estimates

For some clients, an hourly rate might be all you need to negotiate. Corporate or tech clients, for example, might hire you for a given amount of time. If you work on books or other finite projects, though, you might also be asked to let the client know how much time you think you will need (or, ultimately, how much you need to be paid for the project overall). Especially with so many people self-publishing these days, and with so many self-publishers new to the process of developing a book, requests for bids are sometimes brief to the point of absurdity. "How much would you charge to edit my book?" I've been asked. "It's 433 pages." I can tell from the e-mail that the same question is going out to numerous editors, and I imagine the potential client is looking for the lowest bid.

Asking an editor to give a bid based on so little information is like asking a house painter to give a quote without showing the house or giving any details of size, condition, or type of paint required. With so many fonts and specifications at the fingertips of every author, even the page count of 433 is meaningless. Are those 433 pages in 10-point English Times single-spaced with narrow margins, or are they 433 pages in 13-point Helvetica double-spaced with wide margins? The difference could be 900 words to 200, with one manuscript more than four times as long as the other. And word count is just the beginning.

The point is this: Never agree to do a job for any given amount without learning more than a page count. If possible, gently advise the client that hiring someone based on such a naïve bid is dangerous, in fact. Before agreeing to a fixed figure for

Keep in Mind

If you are asked to work at a page rate, explain that a quote will be based on standard manuscript pages of 250 words per page. With the variety of fonts today, a page could have 200 words on it or 900 words, so don't be fooled by a low page count. And don't let the client convince you that the work will go quickly because the manuscript has a lot of tables in it with a lot of white space. Your work requires careful thought, and the amount of thought needed might not correspond exactly to the amount of ink on the page.

any job, assess the manuscript and the goals of the client. The client in turn should be assessing the skill and experience you will bring to your work.

To assess the scope of the job and give a good estimate, start by asking questions. Next, ask to see some manuscript. Finally, do a small sample of work to gauge the time required. Whether you plan to bill by the hour or by some other unit, such as the page, you need to be able to judge how much total time the job might take.

Ask Questions

You can't work well and efficiently without understanding the objectives of your client. Ask questions early in the conversation to try to assess the client's goals and expectations. Review any written information to avoid asking for details already provided, and make a list of questions relevant to the specific job before you speak with the client if possible. Although follow-up questions will sometimes be necessary as you learn more about a project, unnecessary repeat calls will annoy the client. See "Questions to Ask When Assessing a Job" for samples.

Questions to Ask When Assessing a Job

Difficulty of a job and time required to do it depend on many factors. Even before you do a sample edit, answers to some preliminary questions might help you assess the job—and might help you determine whether you want to spend time working on a sample at all. Following are some good questions to ask the client early on. Choose from these suggestions or come up with your own questions based on the nature of the project you are considering.

- What is your manuscript about? What is its purpose?
- Who is the anticipated audience?
- What type of edit do you think the manuscript needs?
- What style manual do you use? Do you have a house style guide? A style sheet from a previous editor?

Continued on next page

Continued from previous page

- In what form will you send the manuscript? If in Word, do you want me to use Tracking? If as a PDF, do you want me to use Acrobat to mark up? If not, how do you want me to mark pages and return them to you?

- How many words does the manuscript have? (A page count is not good enough.) Does it have tables? Charts? Notes? A bibliography? Any other special elements?

- Will I resolve queries after I get feedback from the author? Or will you do that? Will I communicate directly with the author?

- What is the author's background? Has the author published before?

- How firm is your deadline?

- *If you are a proofreader:* Has the manuscript been professionally copyedited? If so, will I get a style sheet? Will I be comparing proof against something— an earlier version or a list of data, for example? Or will I read cold?

- *If you are a copyeditor:* What level of copyedit do you want? Do you need me to do fact-checking? If so, what kinds of things do you want checked?

- *If you are a developmental editor:* Will you send the manuscript for a copyedit when I am done?

- *If the manuscript has multiple authors:* Do you want the writing to be in one voice, or do you want to retain distinct voices for your authors?

- *If the client is an author:* Do you expect to seek a traditional publisher, or are you planning to self-publish?

Get Sample Manuscript

Ask for a sample that is representative of the project. If the first chapter is an introduction written in a different style than the rest of the book, choose something from the middle. Or if the first chapter has been reworked much more than the book as a whole, ask for something later in the manuscript. If the book has multiple authors, ask for samples of some of the most and some of the least polished writing.

Work on Sample Pages

For some projects, five to ten pages should give you a good sense of the work. For particularly long or complex projects, you might want to review a larger sample or multiple samples from different parts of the manuscript. Do two passes if that's what you will do on the full manuscript. Keep a style sheet if you are copyediting. Fact-check as you will for the job. Treat the sample as a part of the job, giving it exactly the same attention as you would if you were doing a full edit. Consider how much time you might need to clean up the manuscript after the author responds to queries if that will be a part of your job. Also flip through the entire manuscript if you can to make sure you are aware of all the different elements included.

Estimate Your Service Fee

Early on, figure out what unit you will use for billing. Most freelance editors—but not all—charge by the hour. Some clients require a page or a project rate, and many indexers bill by the indexable page or even by the index entry. Whatever your unit of paid work, get a sense of how many hours the work is likely to take you. Ultimately, whether you quote a rate based on hours or based on some other unit, you need to be paid reasonably for your time.

When you provide your estimate, give a range of likely costs for your work if possible. If you took an hour to edit five sample pages, base your rate on a pace of four to six pages an hour. Don't make the common mistake of assuming you will work more quickly once you get into the job; unexpected obstacles are equally likely to slow you down. Far too many editors have been embarrassed to admit to a pace that seemed slow for a difficult project and then regretted it later; if you underestimate the time you will need, you could be stuck when it comes time to bill. For the top end of your range, pad your time for unexpected problems. Twenty percent might be reasonable.

Project Rate versus Hourly Rate

Many freelance editors prefer to work at an hourly rate; some insist on doing so. This protects the editor if a job takes longer than anticipated or if the client suddenly requires unexpected work while the project is in progress. But some clients object to hourly rates. After all, many manuscripts could be edited endlessly and could probably improve with each new pass—but the client needs to somehow be able to control the budget.

Personally, I like to work with a project rate, as long as that rate is reasonable and I have a chance early on to assess the project and negotiate. It's sometimes difficult to *stop* work, but if I know the limits to the job, and if I manage my work to finish within a reasonable time given the pay, I work better. I feel confident that I am giving the best value possible within the client's limitations.

At least one other longtime freelance editor agrees regarding project versus hourly rates. "I am uninterested in keeping track of my hours," she says. "Many of my freelance colleagues have sophisticated and detailed spreadsheets that tell them how many words per hour certain types of jobs have taken them in the past (so they can estimate with some precision how long a similar job will take). I honestly don't care how much I make an hour as long as I feel the rate is reasonable. I charge by the job."

Other variations in terms of payment are possible, but in the end, all are based on either time or project—and whether you accept a project rate will depend on how much you think you will be paid for your time. A client who pays $500 for a project with 100 pages is really paying $5 per page. An editor who averages 6 pages an hour at $5 per page makes roughly $30 an hour. So the freelancer who accepts that 100-page project for $500 is betting on making $30 an hour. Experiment to find what works best for you, and then decide whether to bend for a client who insists on a different system.

Provide Your Client with an Estimate

If possible, give a range of potential fees and say that you will bill for exact hours. Say, for example, that you will bill at the rate of $30 an hour and that you expect the job to take forty to fifty hours, for a total of $1,200 to $1,500. Tell the client that you will bill for the time actually worked and hope to complete the work for as little as $1,200 but will not bill more than $1,500 unless something unforeseen happens—and then only after further discussion with the client.

Clients like the security of having a cap on cost for your services. If you promise this cap, however, note that you can honor it only if the client has fairly represented the manuscript as a whole. Also reserve the right to renegotiate if circumstances beyond your control affect the time required. You might bill extra if a client presents you with a completely new chapter after you have already edited the original, for example, or if the client expects you to access a file on a company site but gives you the wrong access information, or if a client asks you to do fact-checking that was not originally requested. You cannot bill for extra time if you have computer problems unrelated to the client's work, for example, or if you simply underestimated your time in your eagerness to get the job.

Hidden Work: Why Does the Edit Take So Long?

A potential client was in search of an editor for his two-hundred-page report—due the next day. When I pointed out that a single person could not complete that job overnight, the client was surprised. "I could read it in a few hours," he said.

Reading is not the same thing as editing.

"But it doesn't need much," he said. "My friend has already reviewed it."

Friends are rarely trained editors.

"The last time I had a report edited, the editor billed me for twenty hours," the caller told me, "but she made only a few marks on the pages."

First, how many is "a few"? (It's often more than a dictionary might indicate.) Second, even if there were only a dozen mistakes, the editor needed to check every single word of the manuscript, think about thousands of words, and look up many to spare the author from embarrassment over those twelve errors.

Two hundred pages overnight? No, editing is not the same as reading.

When you give your estimate, do the math for your client. It might be obvious to you that a job that takes forty hours at $30 an hour will cost the client $1,200. But clients don't always think that far. A client comparing hourly rates from different editors might stop listening at $30 and fail to consider the time required. If you say you will charge $50 an hour and that the work will take two weeks (and you plan to work thirty-five hours a week), give the possible grand total of $3,500. Especially if you are working directly with a first-time author who is new to the world of editors and estimates, avoid catching the client off-guard after you have already done the work.

Finally, put your estimate in writing. Even if you do not have a formal contract, make sure you have a record of the communication. If you discuss the rate verbally, follow up with an e-mail to verify your understanding. Don't assume that the client agrees just because you have given the numbers and the manuscript has landed in your box. Ask the client to confirm receipt and acceptance of your estimate.

Adjust Your Initial Estimate If Necessary

If you have time, return your sample and get feedback from the client before you move ahead with the full project. This gives the client a chance to request more or less work from you. Self-publishing authors sometimes want to rush things, but try to persuade them to take the time for this step to make sure they will get the work they want. Make it clear that you want them to be happy with your work and that the result will be best if you agree to expectations in the beginning.

If the client says your estimate is too high, you can

1. point out examples of time-consuming improvements and try to convince the client that the manuscript will benefit from your careful work as estimated,
2. agree to bill for less time and hope you can work faster,
3. determine that you aren't right for the job and walk away from it, or
4. discuss options for bringing the cost down.

I won't elaborate on the first three options. For the fourth option, though, you might decrease the time you need in a number of ways. If you are a copyeditor, you could offer to do a lighter level of work than you had hoped and than you believe the manuscript needs. Maybe you can't clean up all of the clumsy passive constructions and awkward transitions, but you can correct objective errors and improve consistency. If you are a developmental editor, you could advise the client regarding major organizational issues without addressing details or rewriting as you had recommended.

In addition, or alternatively, you might suggest that the client do more of the work before handing over the manuscript to you or after you return it. If the manuscript has double spaces between every two sentences, the client might be able to clean those up and save you some time. Someone in-house might be able to fact-check the spellings of species names—or a production editor might resolve queries and clean up the manuscript after the author answers questions.

After your client hears your suggestions for cutting costs and understands the work needed, you might get agreement to your original estimate. Or the client might agree to do some of the work you suggest. In either case, make sure that the two of you understand what you can do and what you cannot do within the limited budget. Again, put your limitations in writing.

Adhere to Your Final Estimate If Possible

If you find that you need more time than you expected after you and your client have agreed to an estimate, think about where you went wrong, and try to learn for the next time. If you simply made a mistake, you probably need to take the loss; a client might not have money to pay more than agreed to, and your contact might not hire you again if you seem untrustworthy. You might say that you will honor your original agreement but that the manuscript actually took more time than expected; in this case, the client might offer to pay you more if you are lucky or at least might adjust expectations for a later project with you or another freelancer. Be careful about how you present this, though: You don't want your client to feel manipulated.

Getting It Right

One of the best proofreaders I know charges one of the lowest rates, sometimes a shock to colleagues. With some twenty years of experience behind her, she still bills just $30 an hour for her expert work on technical books. Why? She has steady work with the book publishers she loves. She spends literally no time marketing. While another editor might charge $40 an hour for thirty hours of paid work and nothing for ten additional hours of unpaid work, this editor charges $30 an hour for forty hours of work. Both make exactly the same amount in a week, and the one with the lower rate never needs to worry about whether she will have work.

If something in the job was unexpected, however—maybe the author's work got sloppy partway through—you might be justified in asking for more time. In this case, raise the issue as soon as you discover the problem, and give examples to illustrate. Make sure the client agrees to cover the extra expense; don't just submit a high bill when all is done. No matter how great your work is, a misled and unprepared client will be unhappy, and your reputation could suffer.

Creating Invoices

After the client has agreed to hire you but before you begin work, determine when you will send invoices. For short jobs, you will probably bill after the work is finished. If you are on call to do work for a client, bill at timed intervals. If you are working on a larger project over time, bill at milestones (after a certain number of chapters, for example) or at intervals of time (maybe every week or two weeks). Don't wait to finish a large job to bill. You probably won't actually see money until several weeks after you bill, so you need to start the process soon. Also, partial billings submitted early for a large project will give your client the opportunity to track the project and alert you if hours are unexpectedly excessive.

Make sure to include the following information on your invoice:

- an invoice number to use as a reference
- the date
- your name and contact information
- the name of the client
- contact information for the client
- the name of the project and details about the work: the title of a section and/or the dates worked
- the service you provided
- the number of units you completed (hours, pages, or a project)
- the rate per unit
- the total
- a list of any expenses to be reimbursed with amounts
- terms of payment

For terms of payment, payable within thirty days is typical. Some clients insist on longer terms—forty-five or even sixty days. You'll need to decide if you want the client enough to agree to these long terms. And some freelancers require faster

INVOICE

INVOICE #111

January 2, 2020

Fr:
Barbara Fuller
Editorial Services
1313 Anywhere Street, Someplace, CA
Phone (999) 999-9999
Email barbarafuller@amail.com

To:
Smith Publishing
1212 Somewhere Avenue, Anyplace, FL

Project:	The Story of This chapters 1–10 work completed December 14–28, 2019
Service:	Copyediting
Hours:	48.50
Rate:	$30/hour
Fee Due:	$1,455
Expenses:	None
TOTAL DUE:	$1,455

Please make check payable to Barbara Fuller.

Payment due in 30 days.

Thank you!

payment and even partial payment in advance or in exchange for the work, particularly when working with unknown individuals. Make sure you work out these details with the client before you take the job, and note terms on the invoice.

Collecting Payment

Ideally, your client will send your check on or before the due date, together with a note of thanks for your great work. Sometimes, though, you will need to chase down your payment. If this happens, start with your assigning editor, who might advocate for you. If not, ask for the name and number of someone in the company's accounts payable department so you can talk directly with that person.

Don't wait long after the payment is due to check up on it. Sadly, invoices sometimes get lost in a paper pile or in cyberspace, and you'll want to find out if that happened sooner rather than later. Be professional as you discuss your payment; anger or whininess never helps a case. Also, although you have a right to insist on prompt payment, you need to keep your reputation as a reasonable businessperson.

Being calm is not the same thing as being passive, however. In your inquiry,

- point out that you need the money so you can pay your bills,
- ask when you might expect to see payment,
- ask if you need to talk with someone else, and/or
- as a last resort, state matter-of-factly that you will need to withhold additional work until you receive payment for what has already been turned in—and then follow through.

If you get information about expected timing for payment, take notes. Then, if you don't receive the check when promised, follow up immediately. Remind your client of the earlier promise and ask for an update. Record directly on the invoice any efforts you make to collect past-due payments, exactly when the payment was finally received, and when you deposited the check or when the payment appeared in your online account. This documentation will remind you of what to expect if you accept repeat work from the client. For a client with a history of paying late, you might insist in the future on advance payment or on a higher rate to compensate for the expected delay. (You would take this measure only for repeat offenders and probably not for a client with a rare bookkeeping error. Also, you might eventually be forced to stop working for the client if the client is not willing to adjust.)

Be aware that larger companies can be the worst about timely payment; they sometimes seem to lack personal concern for those who work for them. To be fair, they also have more red tape and bureaucracy to cut through than smaller groups. Government agencies and universities can be especially frustrating. Keep pressing—always calmly, always offering to contact someone else if appropriate. Again, get the person who hired you to work on your behalf if possible.

Nonpayment is rare. Late payment is common. Don't depend on getting your money on time—but don't sit back and accept tardy pay, either. Your client wouldn't be happy if you turned a job in late, and you have a right to insist on timely payment as a professional.

06

Keeping Records and Paying Taxes

How Will You Keep the IRS Happy?

If you are one of more than 140 million Americans who filed an individual income tax return in recent years[1] and you did the paperwork yourself, you might think you can continue the process even after you start your home-based business. And you might be right. I have always filled out and submitted my own forms. But unlike some of my editor friends, I enjoy working with numbers and find an odd satisfaction in puzzling through the many government forms each year. Perhaps even more important, for nearly two decades after I started my business, my accountant-mother would answer any questions I asked or help me find the answers if she didn't have them for me. For many years, I could depend on her knowledge of current tax law, always changing, and on her guidance in sorting through IRS instructions if needed. Without her, I probably would have hired someone from the beginning.

When I first looked at Schedule C, the form on which to report profit or loss from business, I balked at the idea of tackling my own taxes. The form was intimidating. But my mother helped me make my decision: Taking the time to fill out the forms each year, she said, would force me to understand what taxes are all about and therefore to keep better records.

She was right. I do benefit from understanding. Whether you file your own taxes or have someone else file them for you, understanding the process will be valuable throughout the year. On the other hand, because I lack confidence, I still tend to overpay whenever I am in doubt about something. I suspect that I might have saved myself hundreds of dollars—probably thousands through the years—had I hired an accountant. I suspect the fees to hire a professional

---

1   Internal Revenue Service, *2011 IRS Data Book*, www.irs.gov/pub/irs-soi/11databk.pdf.

would have come back to me in refunds. If I were starting now, I would look at it this way: An accountant might hire me to edit a website, and I might hire the accountant to do what the accountant does. It's all about good professional practice.

Regardless of whether you fill out and file your own tax forms or pay someone else to do it, a basic understanding of business expenses and tax write-offs will help you organize and track what you do, and this in turn will make you a better businessperson. This chapter is intended to start you toward that basic understanding.

Preparing Tax Forms

As a sole proprietor with a home-based business, you will need to submit along with federal Form 1040 a Schedule C, "Profit or Loss from Business." You will also fill out and submit Schedule SE, "Self-Employment Tax," and possibly Form 8829, "Expenses for Business Use of Your Home." When you file your taxes or shortly thereafter, you will need to complete Form 1040-ES, "Estimated Tax for Individuals," so you will know how much money to send to the government during the upcoming year.

This section is intended to help home-based editors—particularly sole proprietors—think about tracking income and expenses and organizing records throughout the year so they will be ready come tax time. Remember, though: I am not an accountant. I am an editor. A professional tax consultant can help ensure that you do not overlook anything, particularly in your first years, or deduct something you shouldn't deduct. Furthermore, information here regards taxes for the 2012 tax year and is subject to change. A professional will be informed about current tax laws, always evolving.

View this basic information only as a starting point, then, and a look at some of the most common issues of potential interest to home-based editors. It is intended to increase your awareness but not to instruct you for your specific situation at any given time. If your situation is complex—if you use a business structure other than sole proprietor or if you have employees—it is even more important that you seek professional advice.

Completing and Filing the Forms Yourself

If you are used to filing your own tax forms, you will find at least three big differences when you file as a sole proprietor. First, you will submit Schedule C, on which you will record your gross income from freelance work, subtract your business expenses, and report the difference as your net profit subject to taxes or as your net loss. Second, you will need to calculate your self-employment tax and pay that along with your federal income tax, using Schedule SE to determine the amount. Finally, you will need to estimate taxes for the upcoming year using the IRS Estimated Tax Worksheet and prepay those taxes in quarterly installments on or before April 15, June 15, September 15, and January 15 (or close business days, as determined by the IRS).

Especially if you intend to file your own taxes, take a look at IRS publication 583, *Starting a Business and Keeping Records*; IRS publication 334, *Tax Guide for Small Business*; IRS publication 535, Business Expenses; and IRS publication 587, *Business Use of Your Home*. You can download these documents and others relevant to you from the IRS website forms and publications page (www.irs.gov/formspubs). To get additional help, access the IRS website at www.irs.gov; call IRS telephone assistance for individuals at 1-800-829-1040 or for businesses at 1-800-829-4933; or find your closest taxpayer assistance office for a face-to-face meeting by using the office locator at www.irs.gov/uac/Contact-Your-Local-IRS-Office-1.

Using a Computer Program

With so many do-it-yourself products on the software market, it's becoming easier to prepare your own taxes all the time. Tax programs often come with online chat options and other resources for getting questions answered. Up-to-date programs typically fill the shelves in computer stores at or before the start of each year. If you use one of these programs, make sure you get a current version for home and business (with Schedule C included); the free programs that you can download might not meet your needs. Get a program that offers support and that will guide you through the process, prompting you with questions specific to your situation. A good program will download changes in the tax law as they occur, check your forms from previous years and download relevant information, import 1099s and other forms, do your math, and alert you if you have entered an apparent error. You can typically file taxes electronically using these programs, often leading to a faster refund if you have one coming. Audit support and/or tax consultation might be included in the cost or be available for an additional fee.

If you still do taxes on paper, consider shifting to a software product. You will be surprised at how easy the process becomes, and you are likely to find at least one write-off that you might have overlooked in your paper days, even if your math has always been perfect.

Be aware, though, that tax software is not perfect. Accountants point out that even sophisticated programs sometimes miss subtleties in a business or personal situation that could lead to costly errors or omissions. Check to see if your program provides any guarantee or support to back you in case of a problem—and realize that no formulaic program will be as personal as a good accountant sitting with you at a table.

Hiring an Accountant

If you decide to hire an accountant to help you with your taxes, look for an enrolled agent (EA), a tax professional licensed by the IRS. Some certified public accountants (CPAs) also prepare taxes. Ask around in your community to find someone who specializes in working with small businesses and independent contractors. If you belong to a local group of editors or a discussion group, ask there for recommendations. An accountant who has worked with other freelance editors is ideal, but if you can't find one with that specialty, try at least to get someone experienced in working with home-based businesses.

Keeping Records

When you sit down with your forms each year at tax time—whether by yourself or with your accountant—the process will be much easier if you have kept careful records throughout the year. Furthermore, if you should be one of the relatively few citizens to have a tax return audited (1.1 percent of individual returns filed in 2010, according to the *2011 IRS Data Book*), you will want to have records where you can find them to support your numbers.

Throughout the year, keep your invoices organized in a file, together with details of payment received. Itemize on each invoice to indicate which payments are for services (taxable) and which are for expenses to be reimbursed (not taxable). If your client requires you to submit materials by overnight express, for example, you might need to pay for that expense up front and then include it on your invoice for reimbursement. Indicate clearly that the amount is expense reimbursement and not income. You will not claim that money as income and thus will not pay taxes on it. Keep a copy of each invoice in your system whether you send the original by snail mail or e-mail.

Also save bank records (both personal and business), paid bills, cancelled checks, credit card statements, and expense receipts for purchases of $75 or more. Carbon copies of checks are adequate, but keep complete information about the payee, the amount of the check, and the date of payment. If you have a separate business account, you can keep notes in a register. If you use a single account for both business and personal expenses, keep a separate notebook or computer document listing just business payments so they are easy to find. A note in the memo line of each check can also help remind you of the details of the payment. If you use online banking, you can print out the checks you need to annotate. Make notes directly on receipts to document purchases of $75 or more, and make sure that smaller expenditures are reasonable for your business and that you have full information about those expenditures as well.

A business calendar separate from a personal calendar can provide a good record of projects, deadlines, and meetings. You can also use this calendar to reconstruct your business history or verify business expenses. Get a calendar that you can save; electronic calendars on cell phones, for example, probably will not provide you with the permanent history you need.

Some editors keep a summary of all business transactions on a computer. Many use a spreadsheet or an accounting program such as Quicken. The important thing is to have a system for tracking income and expenses. Especially if you are a sole proprietor, the IRS does not require you to keep records using a specific system; just make sure your records are complete, logical, and consistent.

How long should you keep records? Keep all tax forms sent to the IRS and the state indefinitely. Other than that, keep records long enough to protect yourself in case of an audit—but not so long that your limited office space fills to the ceiling with paper. In general, keep supporting documentation until the relevant statute of limitations runs out. An accountant can be more specific, or see "How Long Should I Keep Records?" at the IRS website.[2] As long as you have filed your taxes honestly, accountants say, you can probably dispose of most supporting documents (but not tax forms themselves) after seven years. For those who use online banking, most banks keep records of checks for seven years, but contact your bank to verify this practice.

---

2   Internal Revenue Service, "How Long Should I Keep Records?," www.irs.gov/
    Businesses/Small-Businesses-&-Self-Employed/How-long-should-I-keep-
    records%3F.

Schedule C is the defining paperwork for sole proprietors, the record of all you have earned and all you have spent for your home-based business within a year. Here you record your gross income from freelance work in part I, subtract your business expenses as recorded in part II, and come up with the number that represents your net profit or loss. (See page 1 of Schedule C form below.)

SCHEDULE C
(Form 1040)

Department of the Treasury
Internal Revenue Service (99)

Profit or Loss From Business
(Sole Proprietorship)

► **For information on Schedule C and its instructions, go to** *www.irs.gov/schedulec.*
► Attach to Form 1040, 1040NR, or 1041; partnerships generally must file Form 1065.

OMB No. 1545-0074

20**12**

Attachment
Sequence No. 09

Name of proprietor

Social security number (SSN)

A   Principal business or profession, including product or service (see instructions)

B   Enter code from instructions ►

C   Business name. If no separate business name, leave blank.

D   Employer ID number (EIN), (see instr.)

E   Business address (including suite or room no.) ►
City, town or post office, state, and ZIP code

F   Accounting method: (1) ☐ Cash   (2) ☐ Accrual   (3) ☐ Other (specify) ►

G   Did you "materially participate" in the operation of this business during 2012? If "No," see instructions for limit on losses   .   ☐ Yes   ☐ No

H   If you started or acquired this business during 2012, check here   .   .   .   .   ► ☐

I   Did you make any payments in 2012 that would require you to file Form(s) 1099? (see instructions)   .   .   .   .   ☐ Yes   ☐ No

J   If "Yes," did you or will you file required Forms 1099?   .   .   .   .   ☐ Yes   ☐ No

Part I   Income

1	Gross receipts or sales. See instructions for line 1 and check the box if this income was reported to you on Form W-2 and the "Statutory employee" box on that form was checked . . . . ► ☐	1
2	Returns and allowances (see instructions)	2
3	Subtract line 2 from line 1	3
4	Cost of goods sold (from line 42)	4
5	**Gross profit.** Subtract line 4 from line 3	5
6	Other income, including federal and state gasoline or fuel tax credit or refund (see instructions) . . .	6
7	**Gross income.** Add lines 5 and 6 . . . . ►	7

Part II   Expenses   Enter expenses for business use of your home only on line 30.

8	Advertising	8	18	Office expense (see instructions)	18
9	Car and truck expenses (see instructions).	9	19	Pension and profit-sharing plans	19
			20	Rent or lease (see instructions):	
10	Commissions and fees .	10	a	Vehicles, machinery, and equipment	20a
11	Contract labor (see instructions)	11	b	Other business property . . .	20b
12	Depletion	12	21	Repairs and maintenance . . .	21
13	Depreciation and section 179 expense deduction (not included in Part III) (see instructions).	13	22	Supplies (not included in Part III) .	22
			23	Taxes and licenses	23
			24	Travel, meals, and entertainment:	
14	Employee benefit programs (other than on line 19). .	14	a	Travel.	24a
15	Insurance (other than health)	15	b	Deductible meals and entertainment (see instructions) .	24b
16	Interest:		25	Utilities	25
a	Mortgage (paid to banks, etc.)	16a	26	Wages (less employment credits) .	26
b	Other	16b	27a	Other expenses (from line 48) . .	27a
17	Legal and professional services	17	b	**Reserved for future use** . . .	27b

28	**Total expenses** before expenses for business use of home. Add lines 8 through 27a . . . . . ►	28	
29	Tentative profit or (loss). Subtract line 28 from line 7	29	
30	Expenses for business use of your home. Attach **Form 8829.** Do **not** report such expenses elsewhere . .	30	
31	**Net profit or (loss).** Subtract line 30 from line 29. • If a profit, enter on both **Form 1040, line 12** (or **Form 1040NR, line 13**) and on **Schedule SE, line 2.** (If you checked the box on line 1, see instructions). Estates and trusts, enter on **Form 1041, line 3.** • If a loss, you **must** go to line 32.	31	
32	If you have a loss, check the box that describes your investment in this activity (see instructions). • If you checked 32a, enter the loss on both **Form 1040, line 12,** (or **Form 1040NR, line 13**) and on **Schedule SE, line 2.** (If you checked the box on line 1, see the line 31 instructions). Estates and trusts, enter on **Form 1041, line 3.** • If you checked 32b, you **must** attach **Form 6198.** Your loss may be limited.	32a ☐ All investment is at risk. 32b ☐ Some investment is not at risk.	

For Paperwork Reduction Act Notice, see your tax return instructions.   Cat. No. 11334P   Schedule C (Form 1040) 2012

Home-based editors can typically ignore part III of Schedule C for calculating cost of goods sold (for businesses that sell items), and many can also ignore part IV for recording information about a vehicle. Part V is a catchall for other expenses not recorded in earlier parts of the form.

Tracking Income

Record your business income in part I of Schedule C. To double-check your personal records, begin by gathering your invoices, as described earlier in this chapter, and the 1099-MISC Forms you will receive by January 31 of each year. Each client who has paid you $600 or more during the previous year will send you one of these forms as documentation of your nonemployee compensation.

Check the 1099s against your invoices to make sure all are accurate. If you see discrepancies, contact the client immediately. One common explanation is that reimbursement for expenses has been included as income, and this needs to be straightened out before filing. A discrepancy might also occur if a check was mailed to you from a client's office on or just before December 31 but reached you after January 1. In this case, if you are using the cash system of accounting, you will record the amount in the year received, whereas your client will record it in the year paid. If you are using the accrual system, you will record it in the year earned, not necessarily in the year received. Clients will also send copies of 1099s to the government, so make sure you understand any differences and correct any errors if necessary. Try to straighten out problems right away; clients have until the last day of February to send copies of 1099s to the IRS, and it's best to resolve issues before then.

After you have checked all 1099s for accuracy and made sure that you have a 1099 for each client who paid you $600 or more, review your invoices for clients who paid you less than $600. These clients are not required to send you 1099s but might report the payment to the IRS. Add the numbers for these smaller bills together with the numbers on the 1099s and record the total as your gross business income.

Tracking Expenses

Record business expenses in part II of Schedule C. If you have kept track of expenses throughout the year, with records, this will be relatively simple. The trickiest part is knowing what to track. "To be deductible," according to IRS publication 535, "a business expense must be both ordinary and necessary. An ordinary expense is one that is common and accepted in your industry. A necessary expense is one that is helpful and appropriate for your trade or business." The publication goes on to clarify that "an expense does not have to be indispensable to be considered necessary." Following are just some of the most common business expenses to be tracked.

Common Write-Offs for Editors

As a home-based business, you can deduct expenses for business items as well as fees paid for business-related services. These can include investments in items or services to help you develop your skills (such as books or course fees), to market your business (such as ads or professional fees), or to set up your office (such as a chair and bookshelves), as well as supplies and resources needed to do your work (such as pens and toner cartridges). Consult IRS publication 535, *Business Expenses*, or your accountant for details. For large items that you need to depreciate, talk to your accountant, or see publication 583, *Starting a Business and Keeping Records*. See also "Common Business Expenses for Editors" (page 102).

Transportation and Travel

You can write off the expense of travel related directly to your business if and only if you have a home office—in other words, the travel from your primary business location to another place of business (perhaps for a meeting or a day on-site for a client) but not from your home (without an office) to another place of business. If you have been wondering whether to designate a specific space for your home office, this information alone might help you decide.

For public transportation, keep receipts. For automobile expenses, you can choose from two options, as long as you are consistent and don't mix methods.

Standard mileage rate. If you choose to track automobile expenses using this option, you can write off a certain amount for every mile you drive. Keep a log with a record of dates, destinations, and total miles for each trip. Then, when you submit

Common Business Expenses for Editors

Computers and other office machines

Desks and other office furniture

Advertising expenses

Telephone

Phone and Internet services

Professional memberships and commissions

Legal and professional services

Training

Supplies and materials (paper, pencils, toner, etc.)

Books

Rent, repairs, and maintenance of equipment

Some taxes (including 50 percent of self-employment taxes)

License

Business-related travel expenses

Business-related meals

Office-related expenses as a percentage of the home:

    Mortgage interest or rent

    Real estate taxes

    Home or renter's insurance

    Utilities

    Maintenance (for office space only)

taxes, take a deduction on Schedule C for total work-related mileage times the flat fee designated at the time. The government determines this flat fee, or standard mileage rate, based on an annual study of the costs of operating a vehicle. In 2012, the amount was 55.5 cents per mile, so someone who drove five hundred miles to and from other clients and meetings during the year could write off $277.50 in travel expenses (500 x .555). Add to that any actual expenses for parking or tolls specifically for business travel.

Figuring transportation expenses using the *standard mileage rate* is simpler than using the *actual expense* method and does not require as much record keeping. Simply keep a careful record of miles driven, together with parking and toll fees. Check your tax instructions for the current allowance.

Actual expenses. To use this method, keep track of payments for expenses such as gas and oil, garage rent, insurance, license, registration, repairs, tires, and lease payment, as well as vehicle depreciation. Also keep track of total miles driven in a year (by checking the odometer on January 1 every year) and miles driven for business (based on a log of business mileage). Then determine your mileage for business purposes as a percentage of your total mileage. If you drive five hundred miles for business and ten thousand miles total in a year, then 5 percent of your transportation costs are for business and can be written off. In addition, you can write off fees specific to travel for business, such as parking and tolls.

This actual expense method requires more bookkeeping than use of the standard mileage rate. It might work in your favor if you had high vehicle expenses, such as a lease and a parking permit, however, and if the percentage of vehicle use for your business were high. Those who drive more than 50 percent for business purposes generally benefit from the actual expense method, whereas those who drive less than 50 percent for business benefit from the standard mileage method. Most home-based editors travel relatively little and prefer the standard mileage rate. Talk to an accountant if you think your situation is unusual.

The Home-Based Office

Business expenses for the home-based office itself can be a significant write-off, depending on the size of your office and its proportion to your home. To claim part of your home as a business office, you must

- use the space exclusively and regularly as your principal place of business,
- use the space exclusively and regularly to meet or deal with clients, and/or
- have a detached space in a separate structure from your living space.

The "office" can be a complete room or part of a room that is separate and identifiable, such as a table and a chair; the space does not need to be separated from the rest of the room by a permanent partition. For the space to be considered "exclusive," you must use it only for your business. For use to be "regular," you must use the office on an ongoing basis, not just occasionally.

Following are examples of ways of conducting business in the home. Some of these spaces can be written off as a business expense, but others cannot.

- **Example 1:** You have your desk, a file cabinet, and a bookshelf in a spare bedroom in your home. In the same bedroom are a television and a sewing machine; you retreat to this space whenever you want time apart from your family. You do not use this room exclusively for your business and therefore cannot consider the entire room to be your office. If you use your desk, cabinet, and bookshelf only for business, you can claim the space that contains those items.

- **Example 2:** You have an Apple computer in the living room where your children can use it for schoolwork if needed. You also have a separate office with a PC and other business supplies. You typically work in your separate office, but one of your clients requires you to use your Mac once a year to work on a publication using a Mac-specific program. You use the office only for work. The separate office qualifies as a business expense, but the desk in the living room does not.

- **Example 3:** You are a home-based editor but have one corporate client who requires you to work at its company location for several weeks each year. You keep all of your records in a room at your home, you do marketing for new clients in this space, and you use the space when you work for other clients. You have a business-only telephone in the room, and sometimes you work there for weeks on end. You do not use the space for anything else. This is a business office.

- **Example 4:** You work primarily in corporate settings in the offices of your clients. You have a desk in one corner of your living room where you keep all records, a business phone, and a computer. You also keep your personal calendar and family bills at this desk. This small space used for both business and personal bookkeeping is not an office. The phone line and computer, if used only for business, are deductible, however.

After you have determined that a space indeed qualifies as an office for your home-based business, you may write off certain expenses associated with that space, using Form 8829 and adjusting the numbers if you operated your business for only part of the year. To start, find the area of the space and then the percentage of the entire home. Begin by measuring the room or part of a room: If the area is ten feet by twelve feet, for example, your office space is 120 square feet. Next, figure out what percentage of your home is in that space. If the space you use for business is 120 square feet and your home is 2,400 square feet total, then your office is 5 percent of your total living space:

$$[\text{office area}] \div [\text{home area}] = \text{percentage}$$
$$120 \div 2,400 = .05, \text{ or } 5 \text{ percent}$$

You can therefore write off 5 percent of your home-related expenses, including

- mortgage interest or rent
- real estate taxes
- home or renter's insurance
- utilities

You can also write off maintenance specifically for the office space, including maintenance that you pay for in a rented office space. Be sure to keep records and receipts to support the amount deducted. Finally, you might be able to write off depreciation on office use of your home. See an accountant for details.

Rumors that a home office automatically invites an IRS audit are false; anyone operating a home-based business is expected to have a place to work at home. Just make sure your space is proportionate to the size of your business and within guidelines. As for all tax purposes, keep records of expenses.

Paying Self-Employment Taxes

Just as all employees join forces with their employers to pay taxes each year toward Social Security and Medicare, independent freelancers who earn $400 or more during a calendar year must also pay those taxes. In most years, the taxes for employees add up to 15.3 percent of net income (up to $110,100 in 2012), with employee and employer each contributing 7.65 percent. Self-employed workers are responsible for the full 15.3 percent themselves, however, to be paid as a single self-employment tax.

To determine your taxable income and pay your self-employment tax, you must submit Schedule SE with your Form 1040. (See Schedule SE form on page 106.) Fill out the form carefully, or have your tax preparer do it; follow form instructions carefully to compute the precise amount. After you figure the amount, write it in as a tax payment under "Other Taxes" on Form 1040. As a small consolation, you can also deduct half of the amount when calculating your adjusted gross income.

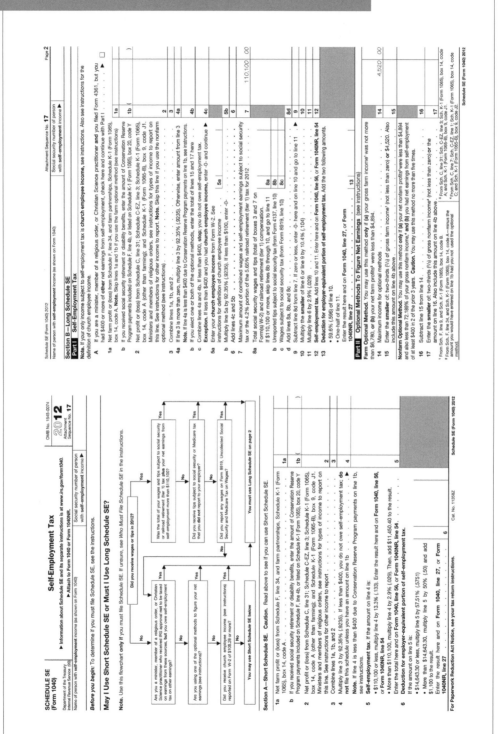

Paying Estimated Taxes

As an independent contractor, you have no employer to deduct taxes from your paychecks throughout the year. Just as an employee, however, you must pay taxes as you earn the money; you cannot wait until the end of the year to do so. To avoid paying penalties, sole proprietors who expect to owe $1,000 or more in taxes must pay estimated amounts using IRS Form 1040-ES ("Estimated Tax for Individuals") four times a year: roughly April 15, June 15, September 15, and January 15 (with adjustments when payment dates fall on weekends). Then, when you file your annual taxes for the year, you will need to pay additional taxes owed, or you will be able to request a refund for an overpayment, just as if an employer had withheld and submitted taxes for you. If you have calculated correctly, any amount owed will be small enough to avoid a penalty.

You can choose one of two options to figure out how much to pay. First, the simplest method is to pay at least as much as you paid in taxes the previous year (including income taxes and self-employment taxes, federal and state). This is the safest way to avoid a penalty for underpayment and typically works best for freelancers, who cannot always control or foresee fluctuations in annual income.

The second method is more complicated but also more accurate and is preferable if you can predict a substantial change in income. For this method, you use the Estimated Tax Worksheet to calculate anticipated taxes for the upcoming year (part of Form 1040-ES; see page 108) and make payments based on that calculation. This might be a better choice if your income is uneven. For example, you might owe fewer taxes one year than for the previous year because you lost a major client, because you have an additional write-off for college expenses for a dependent, or because you gave birth to twins (two new dependents, in addition to time off). In these cases, you might want to hang on to more of your money rather than pay it in taxes only to get a refund later. Or your income might be significantly higher than in the previous year—for example, if you gained a new large client at the end of the previous year or if you hadn't worked the full year before. In these cases, you would be safe to pay at least what you paid the previous year, but you might want to calculate more accurate quarterly taxes and avoid a large payment due in April. In any case, if you underestimate the amount to be paid, you could be penalized.

After you figure out the total estimated taxes you will need to pay, divide the number by four and pay one-quarter of those taxes at each payment period (adjusted for tax overpayments from a previous year if any). If you are paying based

2012 Estimated Tax Worksheet

Keep for Your Records

1	Adjusted gross income you expect in 2012 (see instructions)	**1**
2	• If you plan to itemize deductions, enter the estimated total of your itemized deductions. ⎫	
	• If you do not plan to itemize deductions, enter your standard deduction. ⎬	**2**
3	Subtract line 2 from line 1.	**3**
4	Exemptions. Multiply $3,800 by the number of personal exemptions	**4**
5	Subtract line 4 from line 3.	**5**
6	**Tax.** Figure your tax on the amount on line 5 by using the **2012 Tax Rate Schedules.**	
	Caution: *If you will have qualified dividends or a net capital gain, or expect to exclude or deduct foreign earned income or housing, see chapter 2 of Pub. 505 to figure the tax*	**6**
7	Alternative minimum tax from **Form 6251**	**7**
8	Add lines 6 and 7. Add to this amount any other taxes you expect to include in the total on Form 1040, line 44	**8**
9	Credits (see instructions). **Do not** include any income tax withholding on this line	**9**
10	Subtract line 9 from line 8. If zero or less, enter -0-	**10**
11	Self-employment tax (see instructions)	**11**
12	Other taxes (see instructions)	**12**
13a	Add lines 10 through 12	**13a**
b	Earned income credit, additional child tax credit, fuel tax credit, refundable American opportunity credit, and refundable credits from **Forms 8801** and **8885.**	**13b**
c	**Total 2012 estimated tax.** Subtract line 13b from line 13a. If zero or less, enter -0- . . . ▶	**13c**

14a	Multiply line 13c by 90% (66²/₃% for farmers and fishermen)	**14a**	
b	Required annual payment based on prior year's tax (see instructions) .	**14b**	
c	**Required annual payment to avoid a penalty.** Enter the **smaller** of line 14a or 14b . . . ▶		**14c**

Caution: *Generally, if you do not prepay (through income tax withholding and estimated tax payments) at least the amount on line 14c, you may owe a penalty for not paying enough estimated tax. To avoid a penalty, make sure your estimate on line 13c is as accurate as possible. Even if you pay the required annual payment, you may still owe tax when you file your return. If you prefer, you can pay the amount shown on line 13c. For details, see chapter 2 of Pub. 505.*

15	Income tax withheld and estimated to be withheld during 2012 (including income tax withholding on pensions, annuities, certain deferred income, etc.)	**15**

16a	Subtract line 15 from line 14c	**16a**	
	Is the result zero or less?		
	☐ **Yes.** Stop here. You are not required to make estimated tax payments.		
	☐ **No.** Go to line 16b.		
b	Subtract line 15 from line 13c	**16b**	
	Is the result less than $1,000?		
	☐ **Yes.** Stop here. You are not required to make estimated tax payments.		
	☐ **No.** Go to line 17 to figure your required payment.		
17	If the first payment you are required to make is due April 17, 2012, enter ¼ of line 16a (minus any 2011 overpayment that you are applying to this installment) here, and on your estimated tax payment voucher(s) if you are paying by check or money order.		**17**

on an estimation of your earnings (rather than based on your previous year's payment) and you realize partway through the year that your estimate was wrong, you will need to refigure and alter your payments. If you use this method, you must prepay at least 90 percent of what you owe for the year to avoid a penalty, and you can also be penalized if you do not pay enough taxes for any given payment period. In any case, payments will be due to both the federal government and your state. Mark your calendar to make payments on time each quarter to avoid penalties. Pay early if you like; just don't pay late. You can find payment coupons with your tax forms or submit estimated tax payments online.

The next step, after you estimate taxes owed, is to make sure you have enough money to pay those taxes when they are due. Without cash in the bank, you might find yourself waiting anxiously for a late payment from a client as tax day approaches. The IRS will not forgive you even if your last job did fall through—and even if that last job was for a government client delinquent in pay to you. Taxes are due when they are due. Two good ways to prepare yourself are to (1) divide the total you expect to owe for the year by twelve and put at least that amount in a separate savings account each month or (2) set aside a certain percentage of each check received—maybe 20 percent or more, depending on your individual situation and the advice of your accountant if you have one. After you set aside the money, pretend you don't have it until you submit it to the government.

Paying Use Taxes

When you purchase items from a source that does not collect sales tax, often over the Internet, you must pay use taxes according to the guidelines of your home state. Use tax is the same as sales tax, except that you pay sales tax to the merchant but use tax directly to the state. If you purchase items for your business without paying sales tax, you must report those purchases and pay use taxes once a year to the state or on your personal tax return. For information, check with your state.

How Likely Is an Audit?

Although anxiety about the potential of an audit is always high, the chances of actually facing one are low. For individual income tax returns that include business income (other than farm returns), the 2011 audit rate ranged from 1.3 percent for businesses with gross receipts under $25,000 to 4.3 percent for businesses grossing

$100,000 to under $200,000.[3] Many of the audits that do occur are triggered by losses claimed on Schedule C year after year, by excessively high and disproportionate expenses (especially for a home office, travel, meals, etc.), or by disproportionate contributions to charity, for example. The IRS occasionally conducts random audits as well, but these are relatively rare.

If you are going to get audited, it will probably happen within three years of filing your original tax deposit, so keep your records handy for that time. After that, keep them stored away for a few more years in case you need them; consult with your accountant for a reasonable amount of time. In any case, honest and timely reporting of income and careful tracking of expenses are the best ways to stay out of trouble.

---

3 Internal Revenue Service, *2011 IRS Data Book,* table 9A, www.irs.gov/pub/irs-soi/11databk.pdf.

07

Connecting with Clients

How Do You Find the Clients You Want and Make Sure They Find You?

Many years ago, before I started teaching workshops myself, I attended a program on finding freelance work. John Bergez, a well-established San Francisco Bay Area editor, offered some of the most memorable advice I have heard. In six words, he said simply, "Be a solution, not a problem."

Companies hire freelancers because they need help. Potential clients don't care that you need or want to work on their projects. They care instead about how you can help them. If you call the office of a busy managing editor with a plea for work—maybe because you are a new mother and would like to do something in your spare time or because you need a break from teaching English to high school students—that editor might see you as a problem, as a pesky distraction. The more likable you are, in fact, the bigger the problem might seem.

On the day that you call, the editor might in fact be worried about three books on her desk: three science manuscripts with difficult content in need of a trusted copyeditor. If you had sent a note explaining briefly how you have been impressed by her books, have studied *Chicago,* have a double degree in biology and communications, and would love to contribute to her company's fine work, she might have been interested in what you could do as a solution to her problem—always a better approach.

So how do you get clients to hire you? To build your business, follow these steps:

1. Establish your professionalism. You are a serious, competent person who can do the job well. Show that.
2. Find potential clients. They're everywhere. Some are bound to need your help.
3. Stand above the competition. Convince the client that you can do the job better than anyone else can.
4. Make your client want to hire you again. And/or get your client to refer you to a colleague who needs your help.

This chapter begins with a discussion of step 1, establish your professionalism. After you do that, you can take steps 2, look for appropriate clients, and 3, make sure you stand above the competition. Step 4, make your client want to hire you again, is the subject of chapter 9, "Working with Clients."

Establishing Your Professionalism

As a freelancer, you might never meet many of your clients in person. You will probably communicate with most of them by e-mail and phone long before you trek, eventually if ever, to their office for a face-to-face visit. Dressing and acting professionally for an interview are expected. Even more important in this day, though, is the initial image you project from afar.

Business Cards

With today's electronic communications, you probably don't need fancy stationery; a basic template on your computer with your contact information should suffice. A preprinted business card is another matter, however. You will want something to send in letters or with manuscripts that you return by mail and something to hand out when you connect with others at meetings, workshops, informational interviews—anywhere. A card will provide your potential client with an easy way to keep track of you and your contact information, and a well-designed card can draw attention. If nothing else, a card will send the message, "I am a professional, and I'm ready to work."

If your budget allows it, you can hire a professional to design your card. But if you are starting on a low budget, design your own card at a self-service copy center or through an online business store or print shop. For as little as $10, you can select from templates, colors, and paper styles; add your personal information; and place a minimum order for a couple hundred cards. By the time you use a hundred cards, you will probably be successful enough to order more, or you might have new contact information or other content to include.

Keep the card content simple. Use a clear, easy-to-read font, and place your name so it is prominent. Use your business name and a logo if you have one. Also include contact information (e-mail, phone, alternate phone) and a URL for your website if you have one. Some people include a full address on a business card; others include only a box number or no address at all. As a freelancer, you might not want to give your office (and home) address to every potential client when you are marketing. On the other hand, potential clients who become active clients will want to know where you are. You will need to decide what works best for you. If you've spent $10 on two hundred cards and later decide you should have included your address in a different way, you can try again. Whatever you do, make sure you spell everything correctly and line up everything properly.

Logos

A clever logo will call attention to you when you are unknown and identify you when you are known. A good logo will be easy to recognize and will somehow represent what you do, perhaps incorporating a tool of the trade (a pencil? an edited word?) or perhaps making you stand out through creative use of wording and fonts.

If you are creative yourself, you can find services to help you design a logo at low cost. Type "logo design" into your computer search bar and see what comes up. If you are less creative, you might hire a designer. A professional will discuss your needs and goals and provide you with several mock-ups to choose from. Ask around in your community for a referral. This can be expensive, though—hundreds of dollars. If you have the resources, a logo could be a good addition to your marketing toolkit, but don't borrow money to get one designed; it's not essential.

Telephone Communications

Your neighbors and relatives might have thought the kids on your message machine were cute, but potential clients won't. They're busy people. Your clients want to hear your name so they know they have the right person. Remind them to leave their phone number and, unless your machine automatically stamps messages, the time and date. Other than that, be concise: Potential clients want to leave a quick message and get onto the next thing on their list.

If a client or a potential client leaves a message, call back promptly. Check your messages every morning, late every afternoon, and a few times in between. Set aside a few minutes several times a day just to check and answer messages rather than allowing this task to distract you from other work—but don't neglect communications altogether. If you don't return a call soon, a client might go on to someone else to fill a job. Even a client who says in a message that a job is expected a month in the future will need assurance that you can do it when it's time. And even if you don't need or want the particular job at all, you need to keep the client's respect; you don't want the client to make a mental note that you cannot be trusted for a quick response.

If you are away from your home office for a full day or longer and do not expect to be able to retrieve and return calls, leave a message to indicate that. Don't leave a client waiting for you when you won't be able to return a call. A discouraged client might not give you a chance at all the next time. If the caller can contact you at a different number—maybe a cell phone number—leave that number on your message. Don't answer a business call on a cell phone, though, unless you will be able to focus on the person on the other end when you pick up. Again, clients don't want to fight for your attention.

When you do return a call, always leave a phone number with your message, even if you know the client has it somewhere. Don't make a client work to find you. Speak clearly, and don't ramble.

E-mail Signatures

Set up a signature on your e-mail so it automatically prints every time you send a message. Include your name and contact information—at least your phone number and a website address if you have one. The more prominent you make this information, the more likely someone will use it. A short, clever quote as part of your signature can catch the attention of a client—but keep it short, and keep it clever. Avoid excessive cuteness.

Finding Potential Clients

When you are looking for freelance clients, you can try the traditional routes: Check want ads, job boards, and job lists on the Internet. Don't stop there, though. Successful freelancers use every possible avenue for finding work. When you are self-employed, at least in the beginning, your ability to find clients can be as important as your ability to edit. Following are suggestions to help you with the job search.

Bookstores

If you are interested in working for a book publisher or a consumer magazine, start by browsing local bookstores—not just the big chain stores but also neighborhood stores (if any remain in your area) likely to feature locally published books. Scour the shelves for individual publications or series that interest you. Jot down the names of publishers for later research, and note specific titles and interesting aspects of the books that impress you. Finding publishers in this way has two advantages: (1) you can target companies that might provide interesting work for you and (2) you will have some information about a company so that you can personalize an inquiry regarding work. What better way to impress a publisher than to mention that you have seen and enjoyed some of its work?

Directories

The *Literary Market Place* is a great resource for basic research regarding publishing companies. (See appendix A, "Resources for Editors.") This comprehensive directory includes sections for other potential sources of work as well, such as advertising agencies and book-manufacturing companies. You can find a print edition in the reference section of most public libraries, or access the directory online. A full-year online subscription is prohibitive ($399 a year in 2012), but you can sign up for a shorter subscription at $24.95 a week (also 2012). Choose a week when you have time to research and browse so you can gather and save information.

Once you get online, search the directory for publishers. For example, you can search for all publishers in California. In fall 2012, this search would have turned up 378 hits. With a search for publishers of educational titles in California, the number would have dropped to fifty-five. Professional publishers of educational books in California would have brought up twenty-two hits. Or, as another test, you might have found eleven publishers of fiction in San Francisco and 230 in New York City. One more experiment? Try searching for all of the publishers in your immediate region. If you don't turn up enough possibilities in your hometown, check the larger metropolitan areas near you. If you live in a less populated part of the country, check your entire state.

Why are you doing this? First, although you plan to work from home over the Internet and could work with a publisher halfway around the world, clients often give preference to someone who is relatively local. Some specify that they want free-lancers who live at least within the same time zone.

Second, although you don't need to be an expert in the subject matter for many types of editing, you can demonstrate interest and aptitude if you find content consistent with other things you have done. Have you worked as a nurse? Maybe health care books are for you. A teacher? Try textbooks. Are you an avid backpacker? Who in your area publishes trail guides? For some types of work, in fact, content expertise can be essential—for copyediting of specific genres, such as cookbooks, or for developmental editing. This is often true for the sciences or for any type of technical publication. It can also be true for subjects in the arts. A publisher who needs copyeditors for quilting and needlepoint books, for example, might find that a needlework hobbyist is more likely to spot errors than someone unfamiliar with the craft.

Once you find a publisher through your search, click on the link to pull up the specific page(s) associated with that publisher. Note how many books the publisher puts out in a year. If it publishes only two or three books, the work is probably done in-house or by a single freelancer. If it publishes hundreds of books each year, you might have a better chance for work. Also look for a contact—maybe the name of a managing editor—and jot down a phone number and e-mail address.

Less comprehensive but also a possible source of ideas is a local telephone directory. Look up publishers to see if any are listed. This source might include small companies right in your neighborhood, as well as larger companies. Search for magazines, advertising agencies, biotechnical companies, or whatever else interests you. You won't find more than names of local businesses in this way, but it's a place to start.

News Stories

Watch your newspaper or e-news for stories about local businesses. Might those businesses need your assistance? Maybe they document their products, or market their products, or have shareholders who need information about their products. Or maybe they do research that forms the content for reports. Watch for stories about the top businesses in your region—or about the top businesses in an area of interest to you. Think especially about any that fit your background in some unique way. Did you minor (or major) in environmental science? The environmental engineering company in the next town over might be happy to have you edit its publications. Make a list of potential clients that interest you.

Websites

After you have pulled together a list of clients that interest you (from bookstores or directories or even news articles), continue your research. Check out a company's website as a next step. Remember the publisher who published those beautiful gardening books you saw at the local bookstore? Or the publisher of science textbooks that caught your eye in *Literary Market Place?* Or that name you found under "Magazines" in your local phone directory? Search for it on the web. Most companies have their own websites now, and you can easily learn more about the company. You might also find contact information and even specific information about working for the company. Some publishers provide information about applying for freelance work right on their sites.

Editorial Associations

If you are fortunate enough to live in an area populated by editors, find a local editorial group such as Bay Area Editors' Forum in San Francisco, Northwest Independent Editors Guild in Seattle, or Editorial Freelancers Association in New York and with chapters throughout the country. Some groups have requirements for joining. My own group, Editcetera, selects members who demonstrate strong skills through tests, samples, and references. Many other groups, such as Bay Area Editors' Forum, are open to any individual who pays a small fee. Still others provide free networking and information on their websites. Search the Internet for groups in your area, ask professionals you know for suggestions, or look into joining one of the groups listed in appendix A.

Some of these organizations are general, for any interested publishing professionals. Others are more specific. As just a few of many examples, you might be interested in the American Society for Indexing, International Association of Business Communicators, Society for Technical Communication, or American Medical Writers Association (also for medical editors). While these four groups are all national, each has local chapters as well.

As a freelancer, you need to seek out a community of support, and membership in professional organizations can help you develop that community. Even if the managing editor sitting next to you at an event does not need your services, he might suggest someone who does. And even if the freelancer on the other side of you is your direct competition, she might need to refer someone when she has a surplus of work, or he could be a developmental editor with a favorite client in need of a copyeditor.

Attendance at programs sponsored by these groups is ideal, but even if you cannot participate live, you might benefit from shared resources. Many organizations post job banks on their sites and/or facilitate discussion groups. Some job banks are available for anyone to view; you just need to log on. For others, you need to be a member to have access. Groups requiring a membership fee have a smaller pool of potential applicants for the jobs they post, but choose wisely and join the organizations that best match your interests. See appendix A for more about organizations to consider, and browse the Internet for groups in your area. Whether you find a free job list or pay to join a group with a list for members only, check the job bank regularly. Persistence is important. Don't get discouraged if it takes you awhile to land your first job.

Writers' groups and self-publishing groups, though not specifically for editors, could also be good sources for contacts. Look at adult education listings for your community or check the community boards in a local library. You might attend some

Advice from a Freelancer

"Find yourself a mentor, somebody who knows the business and is willing to advise you. Be flexible—do whatever you need to do (in terms of accepting work that you're not excited about) to get your foot in the door."—A San Francisco Bay Area Editor of these meetings just to get to know people. If you have expertise, you might even line up a speaking engagement—a great way to get yourself known and build credibility. Some groups pay a small stipend to speakers, but even more important, you will be making contacts.

Informational Interviews

Are you interested in obtaining work in the technical industry but unsure about your qualifications? If you were to call a company and ask for a job, you would be a problem; whoever answered would probably tell you sorry, but the company is not hiring. If you were to say instead that you were interested in finding out about editorial work for a technical company, however, you might be able to get an informational interview. This kind of interview is considered educational, and that same overworked manager who did not have time for you earlier might be flattered that you consider her an expert in the field. Ask if you could have just a few minutes of her time—face to face, ideally, but over the phone if that's more convenient. Be prepared to meet at any time suggested, and respect time limitations if given.

If you can get the name of a managing editor or a publications manager, start there. If not, start with a human resources manager or an assistant. You might be surprised at who has time for you if you are flexible. Even a head honcho might just be willing to talk with a rookie every now and then. The higher up you get, the better the overview.

Or you might end up talking with someone not much further along than you are. When I was an editorial assistant in my first year of work, the publisher of my company asked me to handle an informational interview he had lined up. He had intended to talk with the woman himself but had a last-minute conflict that took priority. I worried that I could offer little help to the woman. As it turned out, though, I had been hired recently enough that I could relate to her, I already knew more about the business than I had realized, and I was involved with screening freelancers so knew something about that process. For months afterward, every time I heard of an opening in publishing, staff or freelance, I passed the announcement along to the woman who had come to see me. My boss would have been more knowledgeable, but I was better than no one, and I doubt that he would have followed up as I did.

When you begin an informational interview, have a list of questions you would like answered. (See "Possible Questions for an Informational Interview," page 120, for suggestions.) If you get to meet someone in person, take some business cards, maybe one for the front desk and one for your interviewee. Also take a résumé. Whatever you do, though, don't ask for a job, and don't bring out the résumé until the end of the interview (unless asked to do so). Be sincere in your quest for information.

Workshops

If you live near one of the editorial groups already mentioned, look for workshops offered by that group. If not, try a community college, a university extension program, or even an adult education program. Although you can obtain skills through distance learning programs as well, live programs are better for networking. Instructors sometimes share job announcements with students, sometimes even after a class has ended if a student seems promising. Students also sometimes share job leads among themselves. Don't sit shyly in a corner with a book during breaks; use every minute to get to know others in your community.

Want Ads

As a new graduate looking for a job in the mid-1980s, I was advised not to waste time responding to want ads. Those ads bring thousands of applicants each, I was told, and they would just waste my time. But I had time only to job search and couldn't see the harm—so I followed every possible lead. In the beginning of that summer, I sent off many cover letters and résumés and received no bites. But by the end of the summer, I had refined my process, and in my last week of searching, I heard back regarding four potential positions—including the job I took—all initially found through want ads.

What I had figured out applies whether you are interested in employment or freelance work. Whether you are answering a newspaper ad, an ad on Craigslist, or an ad you see somewhere else, keep in mind the following:

- Respond the first day you see the ad. You might be too late if you collect ads until a convenient time to respond, even if only a few days later.
- Read the ad carefully and show in your application how you will meet the client's precise needs. If the client is looking for a proofreader and you have proofreading skills, highlight those skills. Forget about the developmental skills that you'd rather put to use.
- If you are especially interested in the job and the client has not responded to your application, follow up. Write a simple note asking if you could send any additional materials or answer any questions. Express again your interest, and thank the recipient for the time. Don't be demanding or ask for explanations if you didn't get the job; just make sure someone knows how interested you are. Sometimes a schedule has slipped and the job is still open, or sometimes a client has selected a freelancer who later backs out, again opening the job for you.

For possible leads, try looking for ads under "proofreading," "copyediting," "editing," "indexing," "publications," "communications," and any other headings you can think of. If you are an editor but not a proofreader, look under "proofreading" anyway. Many nontraditional publishers don't know the difference. But beware: Anyone can look for and hire an editor. If you respond to an ad from an independent author, make sure you set your boundaries and act professionally. See "Working with Independent Authors" in chapter 9, "Working with Clients," for more on this issue.

Social Media

Facebook, LinkedIn, and other social media can provide great avenues for networking and marketing. We will discuss social media in chapter 8, "Using the Internet."

Standing above the Competition

Once you have located your ideal client, how do you make yourself stand out among the many editors competing for the work? One way is simply to be known. Another is to demonstrate your skill and experience.

Editors who are shy or solitary (and there are many) might be discouraged to hear that you must be known. Editing tends to be an intellectual business that happens mostly in the head and on paper. But building a business is a different matter. Networking can be just as important to your success as is superior grammar. How do you network? The following should sound familiar to you by now:

- Join editorial associations.
- Ask for informational interviews.
- Participate in workshops.
- Use social media.

We have already discussed these, but the point here is to remember that potential clients will be assessing you in these settings just as you are assessing them. Even if they are not looking for assistance when they meet you, they might remember you later when they do need help. In addition, you might use the following to convince a client of your competence:

- cover letters
- résumés
- project lists
- tests
- samples
- a website
- interviews
- volunteerism and internships

Keep in Mind

A good cover letter gets a client to look at your résumé. A good résumé gets a client to give you a test and/or an interview. A successful test and/or interview gets a client to hire you. Exceptional work on one job gets a client to hire you for another.

Every time you use one of these tools in your job search, you make an impression, good or bad. Make sure the impression is good.

Cover Letters

The cover letter is your first chance to make an impression, the thing that gets a client to look at your résumé. This self-introduction should be concise but strong.

- Address your letter to the proper person, not to a generic someone. If you are answering an ad, look for the desired recipient.
- Show that you know something about the specific client. Do your homework.
- Explain what you can do for the client, not what the client can do for you.
- Say enough to make your point but not so much as to bore your audience. Be specific but succinct.

Over the years, I have occasionally asked managing editors to share with me (and therefore with my students) things that made them want to follow up with an applicant—or not. Specifically about cover letters and résumés, Marilyn Schwartz, former managing editor of the University of California Press, wrote the following:

An application letter and résumé can tell . . . a lot . . . about an applicant. A surprising number of letters and résumés contain basic errors or more subtle defects—e.g., lack of parallelism in list-style entries on the résumé—which seem rather shocking in applications for editorial work. . . . Even when application letters are error-free, they often seem stilted and formulaic, and they fail to address the specifics on the job description. The most outstanding letters demonstrate the individual's personality . . . and self-confidence, as well as knowledge of and interest in [our company] and its books. These characteristics are not stiff or fabricated; the genuineness shines through the writing and presentation, which are individualized. It is rather rare to receive such letters and résumés; when I do, they stand out.

Another editorial manager wrote this:

I like to see some humor in the cover letter. This may not necessarily indicate editing ability, but it does show a bit of the editor's personality and leads me to believe the person will be easy to work with. And personalizing the cover letter to the job listing also stands out—generic cover letters are easy to spot and easy to ignore.

My biggest pet peeve in a cover letter (and especially e-mail cover letters): spelling/grammar errors. Seems basic, right? Well, errors appear, especially when the cover letter is the e-mail. I excuse some of this for production hires but an editor's resume is held to higher standards.

I've intentionally left the repetition in comments from these two editors to emphasize the points.

Résumés

A successful résumé is what gets you to the test, sample, and/or interview. The résumé you present needs to indicate immediately what you could do to help the client and give a sense of why you would do a better job than someone else. Always put yourself in the position of a client who is looking for help, and make clear how you could provide that help. Note experience that relates specifically to the job or the client, including relevant training, courses, and certificates.

Don't try to make your résumé look fancy. "I want to be able to find information quickly, not look at some ground-breaking design," one managing editor told me, emphasizing her preference for simplicity. "Tons of fonts and frills in a resume are a little distracting."

Start with a basic résumé. Keep it on your computer, and adapt it as needed for individual clients. Many editors have variations depending on the type of potential client, type of skills needed, or subject matter. It's important to match the résumé to the job. Someone looking for a proofreader might not think you are the right person if your résumé highlights your copyediting experience and minimizes proofreading. Someone hiring you to work on a travel book might be turned off by a résumé that emphasizes work in education. And although you might be happy editing advertisements and qualified to do so, a résumé that shows mostly book experience will not convince the client.

For more suggestions for writing an effective résumé, see "Tips for Preparing a Résumé" (page 125).

If you adapt your résumé at the last minute for a specific job, be sure to proofread carefully; it's easy to introduce errors when you make quick changes. Make sure your spacing is still correct, your wording is parallel, and your punctuation is consistent.

❏ Make contact information clear and easy to find. Be sure it's correct and current.

❏ Include details of specific skills, experience, education, and awards.

❏ Design your résumé to be attractive but not excessive. Use a maximum of two fonts, one for heads and one for content. Use at least 11-point type. Avoid all caps.

❏ Be consistent. Spell *copy editor* or *copyeditor* consistently, use dashes and colons consistently, use boldface and italics consistently, use (or don't use) a series comma consistently, etc.

❏ Use proper verb tense: past, present, or future.

❏ Use parallel construction within lists.

❏ Customize your résumé for the specific job.

❏ Copyedit. Proofread. Copyedit again. Proofread again. Have someone else proofread for you.

❏ If sending hard copy, print on white or a neutral color. For more than one page, staple the left corner.

❏ If sending via e-mail, use standard fonts. Send a PDF. Use your name in the file name.

As an editor, you get no second chances. If you spell *copyeditor* as a closed word one time and an open word (*copy editor*) the next, the potential client might stop reading right there.

If you have time, back away from your résumé for a while and then review it with fresh eyes. Have a friend read it, use zoom to enlarge the image on your computer, and/or print it out for a final read. No matter how much experience you have and how brilliant you are, a misspelled word, even if it's an obvious typo, will put you in the "No Pile." Poor writing, grammatical errors, and inconsistencies in terms of style will do the same.

Whenever you construct a new résumé or a variation of a résumé, then, keep two important points in mind:

1. Focus on your goal: to convince a potential client that you can do the job needed.

2. Demonstrate your skill. Edit and proofread to perfection.

Careless Mistakes:
The Number One Reason for Landing in the No Pile

Typos in your cover letter or résumé? Careless grammar mistakes? Research shows that applications with such errors are sure to land in the No Pile—and managing editors of publishing businesses are emphatic about the point. Especially if you are applying for editorial work, you can't afford to make sloppy mistakes like the following, all from actual letters of application:

- I am interesting in proofreading and copyediting for you. I am a freelance editor with extensive experience.

- Enclosed is my application for free-lance work. Every client I have had has asked me to work with them again after seeing my work.

- I would like to submit my resume to your company for review. I am agree lance Journalist and writer, among other things. (This one arrived by e-mail. I suspect the sender used a voice recognition program and neglected to proofread before sending.)

Any of these applicants who had taken five minutes to proofread probably would have been horrified by the mistakes. But because the editors rushed, they ended their chances for work before a manager ever looked at a résumé.

Project Lists

For editorial work, a list of completed projects attached to the résumé or sent along with it can give details of your work experience. Depending on the type of work you do, arrange the list by skill, by subject matter, or chronologically. Follow standard style for listing publications; a carelessly constructed project list can do as much damage as good if it demonstrates your inability to pay attention to details. If appropriate, and if you have enough experience, compile and have on file several different lists to emphasize specific aspects of your background.

Tests

Some clients require that editors take a test to qualify for freelance work, either at home or on-site. If you take a test, read the instructions carefully. You might be asked to use specific resources (a certain edition of a style manual or dictionary, for example) or to mark queries in a particular way. Make sure you copyedit if asked to copyedit, proofread if asked to proofread, provide a substantive edit if asked to do that. Doing too much is just as likely to land you in the No Pile as doing too little. If you are to take a test on-site, ask if you should bring any particular resources with you.

If you are taking the test at home and you are asked to mark hard copy, make a copy of the test first so you have the original unmarked version in case you need to start over. If you have an electronic test, make a copy on your computer before beginning work so you can go back to the original if necessary.

In some cases when you work at home, you might be asked to tell how much time you took on a test. If so, take the time to do your best work—but don't take an excessive amount of time. If you are not asked to give the time you took, take as much time as you like. This is a test; you are expected to do your absolute best, and the test is probably rigged with tricks. If possible, let the test sit overnight or longer after you take it and then review it before sending it back.

Think about how you would treat the piece if it were real work (except that you might take longer with it than usual). Would you provide a style sheet when you submit it? If so, do that now. Would you send a note to the author—or to the manager? If so, do that now. Communication with an author is important to the editing process, so demonstrate your ability in that area if appropriate.

If you were given a deadline for returning the test, try to meet it. If the instructions say to ask for more time if you need it, do that if necessary. Most clients would want you to give priority to a paid assignment over a test; simply say that other work has come your way (if that's true). Suggest a later deadline that seems reasonable, and if it's approved, meet that deadline.

After you submit your test, you can check in a day or two later to make sure it was received, but then be patient. Unfortunately, test reviews get relatively low priority in the work queue. If the client has promised results after a certain amount of time, wait until that time has passed, and then ask gently if the client knows when you might expect to hear results. Don't hound.

If you receive a positive answer, be proud; few people pass these tests. Unless you have been asked to take the test for a specific pending job, however, a passing score does not ensure immediate work. Your résumé and test will probably go into a file with the résumés and tests of others who did well so the client can contact one of you when no regular freelancer is available. It could be months before you get work from the client. If you don't hear anything, send a gentle query after a couple of months if you want. Say that you look forward to working with the client and hope you might be able to help with something soon. You can also say that you happen to have a hole in your schedule and would love to help the client with a project if he has one. Then wait some more. Again, don't hound. Eventually something might come your way. The more tests you complete successfully, the sooner something will probably result in work.

For a summary of test-taking tips, see "Tips for Taking a Test" (page 129).

Samples

Another way to prove your ability to a potential client is to provide a sample of your work; you could offer in a cover letter to do this. If you have done similar work for another client, you might submit that as a sample (unless you have signed a nondisclosure agreement). Even better, you could provide a sample of work on the client's own material. Ask the potential client if he has something that you could edit for free to demonstrate your ability. Tell the client that you would want to be paid for your time if your work is used. If not, you will not charge. Consider this marketing.

Individuals, and occasionally other potential clients, sometimes ask a freelancer to provide a sample of work on a pending job. Sometimes the client asks several potential editors to provide samples, with the intention of hiring one. If you are asked to provide a free sample, you will need to decide whether to comply. If you are relatively new to the business and still trying to prove your ability, the time invested might be worthwhile. If you are experienced, you might feel confident that the client

- ❏ Read the instructions carefully. Use the right resources and the correct methods for marking and asking questions.

- ❏ Demonstrate appropriate skills. If asked to proofread, don't copyedit; doing too much is as likely to land you in the No Pile as doing too little.

- ❏ If asked to mark hard copy, make a copy of the test first. If asked to mark up an electronic file, make a copy of the file in case you need to return to the original.

- ❏ Review your work carefully. If possible, let the completed test sit overnight and review it again.

- ❏ Provide support materials if appropriate: e.g., a note to an author and a style sheet.

- ❏ Return the test on time—or ask for an extension if necessary.

- ❏ If you do not receive acknowledgment of your returned test within a few days, check to make sure it arrived with the potential client. Then be patient.

will hire you if you make the effort. In either case, even if you provide this sample initially for free, you might say that you expect to be paid for the work if the client accepts and uses it. If you have all the work you want, you can set a policy of refusing to provide this kind of free sample. But you might lose potential work if you do this, and you might need time to get to this point in your career.

Websites

Many editors today have personal websites where they can post a résumé, a project list, and perhaps samples of work. You can reference such a website on a business card and a résumé and include a link in your e-mail signature. Some of the organizations in appendix A direct clients to the websites of freelancers. We will discuss websites in more detail in chapter 8, "Using the Internet."

Interviews

Home-based editors seeking one-time or occasional projects often sidestep the interview process altogether; the client does not commit to long-term work relationships and so rarely invests the time for an interview. Occasionally, though, especially for a large project or for anticipated repeat work, you will be asked to interview, either in person or by phone. In such a case, keep in mind basic principles of giving an interview:

- Research the company ahead of time.
- Learn what you can in advance about the project. Be prepared to share details of similar work you have done in the past.
- Answer questions directly. Stay focused.
- Project confidence. If possible, explain how you are uniquely well qualified to do the work.
- Follow up. Don't pester, but do drop a note to make sure the client remembers you after the interview. Start with a thank-you for the interview, and end with an offer to provide additional information if needed.

For a personal interview:

- Be on time. Make sure you have directions in advance, and allow time for parking if necessary. If you are using public transit, allow extra time for delays. Plan to arrive fifteen minutes early.
- Dress professionally. Even if casual dress was an original incentive for self-employment, you will need to conform temporarily for an interview. This probably does not mean wearing a business suit, but do dress respectfully, even if the company is casual. After the interview, if you get the job and need to work on-site, take your cues from the permanent employees you will work with.
- Communicate clearly. Shake hands and make eye contact. Speak directly with the person interviewing you. Be polite to others, but don't talk excessively.

For a telephone interview:

- Make sure your line is free at the appointed time. Use a landline if possible for clear communications.
- Clear the room of kids, pets, music, and other distractions.
- Keep your résumé close by for reference if needed.
- Have a pen and paper or an open document ready for taking notes.

"For an interview," one managing editor advises, "I like to feel like the person has done his/her homework and at least looked at our website. I don't expect encyclopedic knowledge of the company, but knowing some of the subjects we cover can go a long way toward making a good impression."

Volunteerism and Internships

Another way to get known and make an impression is through volunteer or intern work. We will discuss these possibilities under "Gaining Experience" in chapter 12, "Developing and Expanding Your Business."

Making Your Clients Want to Hire You Again

After you land a job, make sure you keep your client happy so she will want to hire you again. Getting repeat work is the easiest way to keep busy. It's as simple as that. Second easiest is getting word-of-mouth referrals, which also come from happy clients. So how do you keep your clients happy? Chapter 9, "Working with Clients," suggests strategies. Before we get to that, though, see chapter 8 to learn more about use of the Internet.

08 | Using the Internet

How Do You Make the Most of the Digital Age?

Anyone who does business in the twenty-first century is sure to rely on the Internet. In addition to serving as a tool for research and a means for receiving and delivering work nearly instantaneously, the Internet is a great resource for marketing and communications. Those who get the most out of the Internet use it to

- communicate using e-mail,
- market using a personal website,
- network using social media, and/or
- participate in global discussion groups.

After a discussion of selecting an Internet Service Provider, this chapter will focus on these four functions of the Internet.

Choosing an Internet Service Provider

Before you can access the web or set up an e-mail account, you need to enlist the aid of an Internet Service Provider, a company that connects you to the Internet. If you don't already have an ISP, you will need to determine the type of service you want. The following types of connection are common:

- **Dial up.** Typically the least expensive type of service, sometimes even free, dial up uses an existing telephone line to connect your computer to the Internet. Dial up is the slowest type of service and cannot be used simultaneously with a telephone on the same line. It requires access to landline telephone service and is not an option for a wireless connection. Because of its slow speed, it is a poor choice for a business, even for a small business.

- **DSL (digital subscriber line).** Like dial-up service, a DSL uses an existing telephone line. This service, however, does allow simultaneous use of the line for telephone service. DSL is much faster than dial up, and it can be used for a wireless connection. It is not available in all locations.
- **Cable.** Using a cable television line rather than a telephone line, cable service is much faster than dial up and often faster than DSL, although ranges of speed overlap for cable and DSL. Cable can be used for a wireless connection. Its use is limited to regions with cable.
- **Satellite.** Those who live in areas where DSL and cable are not available, usually in rural regions, might find satellite to be a suitable option. Satellite is available nearly anywhere in the world. It is often the most expensive option, however, and it has limitations: Data delivery is delayed, and weather can affect its use. It is a good choice for businesses only if DSL and cable are not available.
- **3G and 4G (third- and fourth-generation wireless connections).** Less common for computers but used routinely for mobile phones and tablets, 3G and 4G are connections through a provider's cell phone network. These networks allow access from remote locations, even without a Wi-Fi connection. Technology is quickly evolving; by the time this book goes to press, 5G will be common.

Fees for all of these services vary, but in general, the faster the service, the more you pay. As a home-based editor, you will communicate regularly with clients and likely download and upload manuscripts frequently (sometimes large manuscripts), so you probably want to get the fastest service you can reasonably afford. Prices start at about $20 a month for DSL and go up from there. Dial up is less expensive, but it's probably not worth the savings; you might find yourself frustrated if you need to access the Internet while using the telephone, and your clients might become impatient with you even if you are patient with yourself.

When choosing a service provider, be sure you read carefully any agreements before signing. Look for long-term commitment requirements and penalties for changing services. For reviews of ISPs, see www.broadbandreports.com. Although called "DSL Reports," this site accepts and posts reviews of broadband connectivity technology including cable, satellite, and wireless as well as DSL.

You will also need to choose an e-mail service. Ask around in your community for recommendations. Some services are free, but make sure that you get one that can manage volume and large attachments. Also look at reviews regarding both the service and the customer service. If you have a problem when you are working on a job, you will need to be able to get help quickly.

Using E-mail to Communicate

E-mail is likely to be your most common method of communication with your clients. Although just about anyone can log on to a computer and begin sending out messages, those who practice proper business etiquette and manage messages well will present the most professional image.

Writing Professional E-mails

The nature of e-mail communication is informal; most of us have shared messages with friends and relatives that include casual remarks, silly emoticons, and links to jokes that have traveled the world more times than any human alive. The instinct is to keep business communication informal as well—and after you have built a rapport with a client, this might occasionally be appropriate. But until that time, keep your messages professional. And even after you are comfortable with a client, be aware that your message might make its way to some unintended recipient through forwarding or through replies with new cc's.

In addition to using a professional tone, make sure your messages are clear and give the information you want to give:

- Make your main point quickly.
- Use crisp, clear sentences. Readers tend to skim e-mail.
- Use proper grammar, parallel structure, and so on. As a professional editor, be aware that every word you put in writing represents your ability—even in an informal situation.
- Catch your reader's attention with your subject line. A reader who knows you will probably recognize your name in the from line and open the message. But the easier you make it for clients or potential clients to see what the message is about, the better. Ideally, write a subject line that signals the content of the message. Keep it short—to a maximum of fifty characters or so, with the most important words at the start. If you use "From Barbara" or "Hi" as your subject line for every e-mail, a client later searching for correspondence regarding a particular issue might need to open every message

from you to find the correct one. The subject lines "Résumé" and "Project" are little better when a client is searching for something. "Résumé for Fuller" or "Fuller résumé" for one message, "Jones manuscript edit" for another, and "Jones bibliography questions" for a third would enable a client to easily relocate a message if searching for a discussion months after the fact.

- If you are unhappy about something, take special care to monitor your tone. Anger conveyed in an e-mail is permanent. If the situation allows, save a draft of your message and come back to it after you have cooled down to make sure it makes your point without attacking. A later message to ignore the first note can't expunge the damage. A message sent immediately afterward with the subject line RETRACT PREVIOUS MESSAGE (all caps intended) might simply pique the receiver's curiosity. Preventing a recipient from seeing a message after you have hit the send button is impossible, so be careful not to hit that button until you are ready.

- Especially when you are writing to a potential or a relatively new client, proofread and proofread again your e-mails. In some situations, invest the time to copy the content to a Word document and magnify it so you can see every error. Turn on your spell-checker to highlight typos that you might otherwise miss. Everyone makes mistakes occasionally, especially when writing in a rush (as often happens with e-mail communications), but the reader will notice those errors—and readers don't forgive editors who make careless mistakes.

Advice from a Freelancer

"Answer all e-mail correspondence in a courteous and timely fashion, even if it's just a message from an editorial colleague. I'm occasionally in a position to recommend other editors, indexers, or designers. I never recommend people who have poor e-mail etiquette, because it reflects poorly on their people skills and work ethic."—A Freelance Editor

Managing Your E-mail

With the overwhelming amount of e-mail that can land in your box, it's sometimes difficult to get through all of it. Set up a system for management. You might want to have two different e-mail boxes, one for personal correspondence and another for business communications. Your system might also include subject subfolders for messages.

In addition, organize your time; it's easy to get obsessed with e-mail and let it keep you from other important work. If you stop editing every time a bell on your computer notifies you that someone has just reached out to you, you might have difficulty getting anything done. But it's important to review e-mails regularly (at least once every few hours), read professional messages promptly, and let senders know that you have received their messages. If you get a lot of e-mails, try setting aside a few minutes several times a day to look at the messages. If a message requires a response and you don't have time immediately to think about the content, let the sender know you have seen the message and will respond within some amount of time, and then do so.

Likewise, if you have sent an important e-mail message, make sure the client actually got it. If you don't get a timely acknowledgment, check in with the recipient using another e-mail or, if it's really important, a quick phone call. Although we tend to assume that all e-mails reach their destination immediately, messages do occasionally go into spam or junk folders or, rarely, disappear completely into cyberspace. In other situations, a recipient accidentally deletes the message before dealing with it, or a sender finds a message days later trapped in a draft folder or an outbox. Be sure to archive important e-mails in case you need to refer back to the correspondence.

Sharing E-mail with Others

With the ease of sending e-mails, many of us are tempted to share every piece of information with anyone who might possibly be interested. Remember, though, that while you can easily type a few more addresses into a cc line in a few seconds, those on the receiving end actually need to take the time to read the message. Those who receive many unnecessary messages from you might stop looking at them altogether and then overlook something important.

With this in mind, think twice before including a long string of recipients in a cc line. Does everyone really need to see your e-mail? Sometimes the answer is yes, but not always, and it's important to respect the time of others. Also beware of forwarding messages to others after you have received them. Sometimes it's important to pass the information along to someone else, but think about whether you might inadvertently be sharing something confidential or conveying personal information that shouldn't be conveyed.

Using a Website to Market

A website can be useful as a marketing tool to show what you can do. It gives potential clients a way to find you and learn something about you, what you have done in the past, and what you can do for them. Posting information on a website can draw clients to you and also save time for both you and your client by eliminating the need for you to answer basic questions and pull together marketing materials for each new prospect. Some editorial groups encourage members to post websites that can be accessed from the organization site, or you can include links on a résumé or in an e-mail signature to direct potential clients to your site. See appendix A for organizations that might help make your site visible.

Things to Include on a Website

Where do you start? Begin by looking at websites of other editors. See what draws your attention and impresses you. A good editor's website might include some or all of the following:

- A home page. Write something snappy to grab attention—maybe two or three brief paragraphs to give an overview of your experience, your areas of expertise, and any special skills or awards that make you stand out. Make the content punchy and easy to read. If you have a logo, include it. Also make your contact information prominent, either here, on a separate contact page that is easy to find, or both.
- A page (or two separate pages) with a full résumé and a project list. See chapter 7 for more about constructing a résumé. A project list could include details of past experience.
- A page to explain different types of editorial work you do and include or link to a portfolio with samples of past projects. Be sure to get permission to include any actual samples, and be mindful of work for clients with whom you have signed a nondisclosure agreement. If you don't have a real sample to use, try explaining what you do and creating a sample to illustrate.

- A client list. If appropriate, organize your list by type—maybe book clients, corporate clients, health care clients, and so on.

- Testimonials from past clients. Glowing remarks from a happy client can help convince a potential new client of your ability. Make sure you get permission to post quotes from those who have praised your work. If you haven't received written kudos spontaneously, ask clients who have commended you verbally if they would be willing to write something. Many are happy to do so.

- A blog. Providing useful information might draw some of your viewers back to your site, let viewers get to know you, and keep your name fresh in their minds. Writing frequent blogs can be time-consuming, and you must write them professionally and post them error-free. But if you have the skills and the time, this can be a good way to draw attention to yourself. Blogs can also make your site more visible by improving your search ranking; an active site draws more attention.

- A page with frequently asked questions. If you find that you answer the same questions repeatedly for potential clients, include those questions and answers on your site. Beware, though. Some answers probably vary depending on the situation, and you want to publish only policies that will apply to all situations. For example, you might typically charge $30 an hour for copyediting—but under some circumstances, you would want the right to negotiate. And you might typically edit 1,500 words an hour, but again, you probably wouldn't want to commit to that without seeing a particular manuscript and learning more about it.

The Mechanics of Posting a Site

To post a website, you need a domain name registered through a domain registrar. Registration of the domain name is typically inexpensive—as little as $5—and gives you ownership of the name for as long as you continue to pay licensing fees. Your domain name needs to be original, not previously claimed by someone else. It should be short and simple, and others will remember it best if it is the same as or related to your business name. For example, Editcetera uses the domain name www.editcetera .com, the Bay Area Editors' Forum uses www.editorsforum.org, and the Editorial Freelancers Association uses www.the-efa.org.

If you cannot get a recommendation for a registrar from a colleague, search "domain name registrar" on the Internet. You might look for a registrar that also offers a web hosting service (an Internet service that allows individuals and organizations to make their website accessible via the World Wide Web) and even custom-design services. If the registrar you choose will not host your site, look for an Internet Service Provider or another Internet company that can do so.

Once you find a registrar, check to see if your desired domain name has already been claimed. If so, you will need to find an alternative. You could also try the same name with a different extension (such as "net" instead of "com"), but keep in mind that most people automatically assume the use of "com" for domain names and might not find you with a different extension. Whatever company you choose, make sure you retain full ownership of your domain name, and read the fine print in any contract before you sign.

If you have developed websites in the past, you might be able to create your own site now. Even if not, you might find a free service on the Internet or through an organization to help you with the process. Beware, though: Your site is your public image, and you want to be proud of it. A poorly designed site could do as much damage as good for your reputation. Unless you have design skills yourself, therefore, and unless you want to invest many hours to produce what might still be an inferior site in the end, hiring a professional designer might be worth the money spent.

If you decide to hire a professional, get estimates from a few web designers whose work you like. Find out if the designer can help you find a host service and register your domain name; many can, and this might be valuable to you. If your budget is tight, look for a student at a local art school or a community college. A beginner who has studied web design might have enough skills to create a professional site and might be happy to get the experience of working with you for a relatively low rate. Make sure you hire someone who has the ability not only to design but also to post your site and who will then give you access so that you can modify it later yourself.

Tips for Developing Web Content

Keep in mind when you write copy for your site that people read in different ways on the web than in print. Web users want to find information fast, and they often scan content without reading line for line. According to a study by the Nielsen Norman consulting and research group, web users typically read in an F-shaped pattern: They begin at the top left of a page, move across the top, scan down the left edge of the page and across again for a shorter distance, and then continue down the left side of the page. For details, see Jakob Nielsen and Kara Pernice, *Eyetracking Web Usability,* New Riders Press, 2009. Understanding reader habits will help you write and organize your copy.

- Front-load your information. Let people see who you are and what you do immediately when they get to your site.
- Be concise. Although you might include more complex work on sample pages, your home page is a marketing tool and needs to capture the viewer's attention quickly. Especially for this page, limit the content so it can be viewed on a standard computer screen without scrolling. For introductory text, use short paragraphs, short sentences, and small words.
- Make content easy to scan. Draw attention with headings, boldfaced terms, and images. Use lists where appropriate.
- Use keywords that might come up in a search engine. Think about how people might search on the web, and try to incorporate words that a potential client might use. If you say on your site that you provide "editorial services," you might fail to draw attention from clients looking for "proofreaders," "copyeditors," or "developmental editors." "Medical editor" might draw more of your ideal clients than simply "editor." Think about what words you would use to search for an editor with your skills, and plant those words in your copy, in heads if possible. This use of keywords might contradict the concept of concision, but in this case, let the keywords overrule.

Using Social Media to Network

In less than a decade since the introduction of Facebook, use of social media has spread rampantly throughout the world. Free and easy to use, this modern channel of communication facilitates both personal and business outreach with little investment of time. Promoting your services through use of the media is simple and quick.

Facebook

Launched in 2004, Facebook had reached more than a billion users by the end of 2012, making it the largest online social network. In addition to facilitating the personal pages of all of these individuals, Facebook makes available pages for businesses to use for free. As with personal Facebook pages, business users post images (maybe a logo and photos), updates, videos, and questions on their pages, and the posts then appear in the news feed of anyone who has "liked" the business. Different from personal posts, the communication on business pages is one way; posts from those who have liked your business will not appear on your public page. See "Tips for Writing a Facebook Post." To learn more and set up a business page, see www.facebook.com/business.

LinkedIn

Launched in 2003, LinkedIn claims to be the world's largest professional network, with more than two hundred million members at the start of 2013. It is specifically intended for business-to-business (B2B) interactions among suppliers and partners. When you set up a LinkedIn account, you build a profile that includes information about yourself and the service you provide. See "Things to Include on a LinkedIn Page" (page 142) for details. Connections can be used for building resources and learning about job opportunities. You can join a LinkedIn group with common interests, connect to Twitter, and so on . . . and as with other forms of social media, no matter where you or your colleagues go, you can always find each other through this free service. To sign up, go to www.linkedin.com.

> ### Things to Include on a LinkedIn Page
>
> Start your LinkedIn page with your current title (such as Freelance Editor) and place of work. Other possible things to include are
>
> - background summary
> - work history, with descriptions of work done
> - education history
> - skills
> - recommendations
> - contact information
> - connections (shared links)
> - "following" (groups of interest)
>
> Add to your page as you have new information.

Twitter

Launched in 2006, Twitter provides a way for hundreds of millions of people (more than five hundred million registered in 2012) to connect using "tweets," spurts of information limited to 140 characters. The practice of broadcasting these concise messages has become so common since the introduction of Twitter that *Webster's* now includes a definition of *tweet* as "a post made on the Twitter online message service." Each tweet can include a full message or a link to more information. As a business with a Twitter account, you can quickly share information about what you are doing or listen in on the conversations of others in your industry. To join, go to https://twitter.com/signup.

Google+

Launched in June 2011, Google+ had gathered some five hundred million registered users in its first year and a half, by December 2012. Users of Google+ begin with a profile page that includes personal images and information, similar to a Facebook page. Also as for Facebook, Google+ users collect "friends," including personal

acquaintances as well as other individuals of interest, such as journalists or other
editors; as with Facebook business pages and Twitter, users can follow individuals
who interest them without the knowledge of those individuals. Google+ also allows
users to divide friends into "circles." For example, you could have one circle of family
members, one of friends, one of colleagues, and one of clients. After you set up these
networks as circles, you select which circles see which of your posts. To sign up, go
to www.google.com/+.

Participating in Global Discussion Groups

One more direct way to communicate specifically with related professionals, even
predating Facebook, is through discussion groups. Some of the organizations listed
in appendix A sponsor such groups to facilitate communication regarding topics of
interest to editors. Smaller local organizations also sometimes sponsor these groups.
Some involve communications through Yahoo or Google, whereas others are set up
as e-mail lists sometimes generically referred to as "listservs," after LISTSERV (an
e-mail list management software produced by L-Soft).

Editors in discussion groups can raise questions or point others toward useful
information. Content includes, for example, questions about grammar or usage;
links to meaningful articles or blogs; and announcements of relevant publications,
learning opportunities, or even jobs. Depending on the size of the group, you might
find only occasional messages in your box, or you might get dozens of messages
every day. Alternatively, to reduce the activity in your box, you can sometimes elect
to have messages bundled in a single article, called a digest, and delivered in batches.

Do you have a question about grammar? Throw it out for discussion, and
depending on the size of your group, you might get one or a dozen answers within
hours supported by quotes from resources or Internet references. Only a group of

Tips from a Social Networker

Use of social media since 1999 has boosted the career of San Francisco–based editor Geneviève Duboscq. After subscribing to three e-mail groups, Geneviève writes, "several list members I later met in person said they felt like they knew and trusted me because of the information I had posted. For an introvert, this kind of publicity or reach is pure gold."

Geneviève adopted the following guidelines for use in her own work.

For Discussion Groups:

- Post only positive comments, links to interesting materials available on the web, and questions about tricky professional matters (how to negotiate for higher rates, for example, or how to make cold calls to drum up business).

- If you post a question and receive multiple private replies, share the information with the whole group. Thank those who responded. "People like a little public acknowledgment and the sense that they have been helpful to others," Geneviève says.

- Delete posts that you do not want permanently online. Search the Internet for instructions.

For LinkedIn:

- Use the LinkedIn profile as a portable résumé.

- Be honest in your posts. Some human resources departments check references and implied claims scrupulously. Don't say, for example, that you have worked for a major company when in fact you did only a small freelance job for someone who worked for the company. "My guide is Mark Twain," Geneviève says. "'Tell the truth. It's easier to remember.'"

- Remember that discussion lists are searchable. If you regret having posted something after the fact, use a search engine to find out how to delete it.

- Prune contacts periodically: If you can't remember who the person is or how or whether you met, consider deleting that contact.

For Blogs:

- Keep your ideal reader in mind at all times: the future client or employer, for example.

- Write to give a snapshot of who you are, how you think, and what you value.

- Be clear about your goals for your professional blog. Assume that nobody, apart from friends or family, cares how you feel about most things.

- Prune the blog. Regularly check links on old posts to make sure that they still work, and delete posts that have grown stale or have no lasting value.

"Especially for a freelancer, but really for everyone," Geneviève says, "it's important to give others a way to look at you and get the measure of you without requiring that they enter into contact with you. E-mail discussion groups, LinkedIn, and blogs are easy ways to publicize yourself without being phony. It's important to build a public persona and maintain it; that's part of being a professional."

editors could produce fifteen comments over two days about the correct term for the color of skin as a symptom of asthma—or engage in a four-day discussion about the word *spineless* as applied to people. On another level, you might ask a question about business practices. Not sure whether a holiday greeting is appropriate for clients? Ask your colleagues and see what responses you get.

Fifteen years ago, an editor with questions about such issues would have been working in relative isolation, with limited resources to tap. Today, the world is available through a keyboard and an Internet connection.

Lessons Learned

"I wish I had a networking group [when I started out]. It took me several years to grow my network."—Susan Moxley, Editor

09

Working with Clients

Keeping Clients Happy—and Avoiding Trouble

No matter how talented you are as an editor, finding clients and landing jobs depends a lot on business savvy, a lot on networking, and at least a little on luck. Once you get a few clients to give you a chance, though, your business will thrive only if those clients are happy with your work. Ideally, your clients will come back to you with other work opportunities, and if this happens, the ratio of paid-to-unpaid work will go up immediately. But even if a client does not have more projects to keep you busy, you need to leave a good impression when you close a job. Word of mouth—both positive and negative—travels far. If it's positive, it's your best form of marketing.

Years ago, a top-notch proofreader told me about a distressing experience she had working on-site for a client in San Francisco. Although she knew she had saved the company from countless embarrassing and potentially damaging errors, the client was unhappy with her work. She later learned that some of the company employees had been uncomfortable with her manner and with the harshness of her queries. "I guess it doesn't matter how smart you are if they don't like you," she told me bitterly.

She was right. A freelancer by definition is hired temporarily to do a finite job. A client who doesn't like your work *or who doesn't like you* has no obligation to continue working with you. Only clients who like you will rehire you or refer you to colleagues. A client who is dissatisfied could not only turn to another editor for the next project but also make it difficult for you to find work elsewhere in the community.

Applying exceptional skills is the best way to impress your client, and doing that depends on your talents as an editor. If you need ideas for improving or increasing your skills, see chapter 12, "Developing and Expanding Your Business." Beyond that, this chapter addresses work habits and practices that might lead to good client relations. Then, after discussing ways to increase your chances for a positive work experience, we explore signs of potential trouble and difficult clients you might want to avoid.

Increasing Your Chances for Repeat Work

In addition to strong editorial skills, business habits can make a big difference in the impression you make with your client. What makes a client happy?

- a job done well
- a job done on time and within budget
- a freelancer who can do the job with little supervision, leaving the client free to do other work
- an agreeable and pleasant work relationship

Success in these areas requires sound skills, professional and courteous communications, the judgment to ask enough (but not too many) questions, the confidence to move ahead when you have the information you need, and the tact to deal with problems professionally.

Manager Comments: Freelancer Qualities for Success

When asked what might make a manager hire a freelancer to do a second job after some initial work, clients responded with the following:

- initial work that is thorough and meticulous
- ability to follow the instructions provided and to seek clarification if the instructions are not clear
- clear and appropriate queries to the author and to the client
- well-written, diplomatic notes to the author
- positive author feedback

One manager elaborated on the fourth point: "It's not easy to tell an author to rewrite badly written or badly organized copy."

Understanding the Job Requirements

In order to best meet the needs of a project, make sure you understand the various players and components at the outset. Read written instructions and review any materials received. Then, if you do not have all the information you need, ask intelligent questions to get answers quickly without wasting time for your client.

The following sections suggest possible questions to be considered for any job. You might have addressed some of these issues early in the process, when you were deciding whether to take the job and preparing an estimate. But you might not have all the information you need yet.

The trick is in knowing what to ask. If you asked every question listed here for any given job, you would annoy your clients, possibly pushing them to look elsewhere for assistance. "If the questions are intelligent, I usually see them as a sign that the person cares," one managing editor says. "But if the freelancer asks *too* many questions or requires a lot of extra time and attention from me, I might think twice about hiring him or her."

So think about the following aspects of a job, pull together the information you have been given, decide which additional information you need, and ask smart questions to make sure you know how to focus your work.

Understand the Purpose of the Project

What is the purpose of the project? Is it to educate experts in a field? Give laypeople general information? Entertain? Instruct? Sell? The more you know about the intent of the project, the more you will be able to edit to serve the purpose.

Know Something about the Author

Has the author published before? How you phrase queries and explain your work could depend on the author's experience. Is the author a professional writer? An expert in the field? Try to learn what you can about the author from your client or, if your client *is* the author, from your initial interactions. Does the author like explanations about things (and have time to review those explanations), or should you make changes silently whenever possible? If you are working on business materials, will you be editing toward a corporate voice without regard for the author at all? If so, make sure you understand the desired corporate voice. See if you can get examples of successful documents already published.

Know Something about the Intended Audience

Will readers be experts in the field? Laypeople? Consumers? Scholars? Policymakers? Will they expect to learn how to use something or to do something? If so, is that something completely new to them?

Understand the Publisher's Conventions

In some cases, a client might hand over a manuscript and give you the freedom to edit as you like. In other cases, the client has specific guidelines. Which is true for the project at hand? Does the publisher follow *Chicago Style? Associated Press?* Another style guide? Has a particular dictionary been used? Many publishers have a house style guide with records of decisions and preferences. Many businesses—institutions, ad agencies, etc.—also have house style guides. If the house does not have a preferred style manual and dictionary and you are working at a later stage of the process (proofreading, for example), what style has someone else used on the manuscript before you?

Understand the Publisher's Budget

Have you agreed to a cap on the project with the publisher? If so, is that cap rigid? Even the most experienced editors sometimes make the mistake of overworking. But if a publisher has a limited budget, you must stay within that budget. If that seems impossible, discuss the situation with the client early on, decide whether and how you *can* work within the budget, and then adhere to your agreement.

Understand the Process

If you have been asked to work in Word, does the client want to see changes tracked? Does the client expect you to do formatting in addition to editing? Does everyone who will review your work know how to view tracked changes? If not, will you need to explain? If you are developing a manuscript, will you write notes and let the author work from them, or will you continue to work with the author throughout the duration? If you are copyediting, will you review answers to queries and incorporate changes, or will an in-house editor do that?

Question: Are You Expected to Fact-Check?

As an editor, you are not generally expected to be an expert on subject matter; that's the writer's zone. On the other hand, you will be at least somewhat responsible for making sure the content of a publication is correct, not just in terms of grammar but also in terms of factual accuracy. How far does your job extend?

Following are just a few of the types of things you might want to ask about if they appear in your work. These are only examples; every publication has different needs, and you will find many other situations.

- If you are working on a field guide, are you expected to check the scientific names of all species? As a copyeditor, you should check for consistency and logic, but how far do you go beyond that? You *should* be able to depend on a careful author to be accurate, but confirm that with the client. And if you are to check scientific names, what resource should you use?
- If the publication you are working on includes equations, are you expected to check the math? The answer is typically no—but not always.
- If you are working on historical fiction, should you check dates for accuracy—or only for logic? You should always point out illogical sequence (such as a major event in a subject's life that actually occurred before the subject was born), apparent errors (such as an event happening in the wrong century), and so on. But should you double-check dates of events in general?
- If you are working on corporate publications, do you need to check brand names? Probably so. But against what?

Somewhat related, if you are working on a new edition of a previously published book, do you need to review material that is not changing? Many authors say no, but often those authors don't understand the need for internal consistency. All the same, a client with a tight budget might need to limit the work of the editor.

Question: How Flexible Is the Schedule?

For any project to be successful, freelancers must respect the schedule. Sometimes, however, things happen beyond the control of the freelancer. For example, an author submits a manuscript late, which means the copyeditor (or another freelancer in the chain) gets a late start. In this situation, does the freelancer need to rush to stay on schedule, even with a shorter time to work, even if that means taking less care than might be ideal? Or is time available to do the best job possible even if that means pushing out the deadline? Depending on the project and the purpose, extra time might be available and even advisable. For a novel or a cookbook, for example, the publisher might decide to postpone a publication date. The anticipated shelf life of that novel or cookbook might be long, justifying the time to make the publication its absolute best. On the other hand, a cookbook intended to inspire home chefs for the holidays will fail if it hits the market in January instead of November. And for a publication timed to coincide with a meeting, a current event, or the release of a product, missing a deadline could mean that a perfectly edited publication never gets read.

Asking Just the Right Questions—but Not Too Many

No matter how carefully you have prepared for a job, more questions invariably arise after you begin work.

- You discover that the author has begun adding metric equivalents in parentheses for all units of measurement beginning with chapter 4. Should these equivalents be added where they were missing from chapters 1 through 3? Deleted where they exist? Should you simply write a note to the author to add or delete them, or should you do the work yourself? And should you check the conversions already included or trust that the author has calculated them correctly?
- You find that you are rewriting sentences on every page to cast them in a more active voice. Your instructions are to do a medium-level copyedit, and you think this should include revising passive constructions, but you don't think you can meet your budget if you continue at this pace. Should you keep revising? Should you ask the author to revise? Or should you let these sentences stand as they are?
- You find that the author follows British style for such words as *towards* and *colour*. If the author is consistent, should you let her have her way?

- As part of your work, you have been checking citations against notes and looking not only for style problems but also for inconsistencies and apparent errors. The multitude of mistakes you have found makes you think you should check original sources for all notes. You know you could keep your bill lower if you asked the author to do this work—but you don't trust the author to do a good job. What should you do?

These are all legitimate questions. But remember that opening advice to chapter 7: "Be a solution, not a problem." If you pick up the phone and call your client every time a question occurs to you, you create more work than you unload. While you don't want to make the wrong choices, you have been hired to make decisions and to alleviate the client of work.

So what do you do? If something is likely to affect your ability to meet a budget or a schedule, ask about it. Beyond that, use the good judgment and common sense listed in chapter 1 as essential characteristics for an editor. Ask the questions you need to ask—but no more. Make a list of questions that arise over the first couple of days, figure out which ones really require input from your client, and organize yourself to minimize the time required for discussion.

For anything but the shortest of projects, work a few days before you call so you can get a good sense of the job as a whole. You might find that the answers to some questions become clear as you continue your work. If you have questions about whether you should take the time to complete certain tasks, you might realize that moving ahead would be less time-consuming than discussing the issues. For example, maybe there weren't so many missing parenthetical metric conversions in that manuscript after all, and you can fill in the numbers almost as quickly as you could ask someone else to do it. You might also find something in the later text to indicate why those conversions are important and do need to be added in the earlier pages.

Review your questions before you contact your client. Delete any that you can answer yourself. Then request a few minutes of time. Your client will probably appreciate your efforts to get the job right as long as you respect her time. If you continually disrupt her other work, though, she might be more annoyed than impressed, and she might choose to work with someone different the next time around. Keep your discussions positive, always with the idea of working together with the client to achieve the desired goal, always with consideration for her busy schedule.

"I really like someone who can catch on quickly and doesn't require too much hand-holding," one managing editor told me. "Asking questions is one thing, but we have one contractor who bugs us endlessly with questions about things most people would figure out on their own, and she always seems a bit slow. If someone else is available, I use that person instead, even though this gal is a good editor."

Communicating Tactfully with the Author

Another essential characteristic of a good editor as listed in chapter 1 is an ability to communicate tactfully with authors. Keep in mind that you are working with your author to produce the best possible publication; you are not in a battle to determine who is smarter, and you must avoid confrontation. Whether you are writing long memos as part of developmental work or brief queries as a copyeditor, tact is essential. If you alienate your author, your client might alienate you.

Tact, too, is often a matter of common sense. It too comes from experience. You can start with a few basic principles to help keep things positive and constructive, however.

- Keep in mind your goal: to help bring out the best work possible from an author or another client.
- Treat all clients with respect. Recognize their expertise. Remember you are assisting them, not the reverse.
- Avoid sounding pedantic, sarcastic, or argumentative. Also avoid using humor that might be misinterpreted.
- Avoid seeming to question an author's expertise. Point out factual errors if necessary without making personal judgments or accusations.
- Point out strengths in a manuscript. Then, if you find material that is less well written, point to the strong section as an example to be followed for improvement. Even authors who seek out criticism thrive on praise.
- When calling attention to shortcomings, focus on the manuscript and its purpose. Never make a criticism personal. The manuscript falls short, not the author.
- Keep in mind the reader, and phrase suggestions in terms of the reader: "Readers might be confused by this statement, which seems to contradict the earlier suggestion that . . ."

- Be specific. If you aren't sure what an author intends to say, suggest a couple of possibilities and ask which is correct. Even if you fail to suggest the correct interpretation, the author will see why you are confused and better address the problem.
- Especially if you are copyediting, avoid long explanations of your work. Authors might see these as condescending and/or be frustrated at the time required to read your notes. You have been hired to fix the problems. If you are certain that a change is needed, make it and move on.
- Review all queries before submitting your work. You might find that some are unnecessary, some are poorly worded and need clarification, and some need to be revised for better tone.

Poorly written queries can lead to confusion and, in the worst cases, create animosity between editor and author. As a common example of an ineffective query, I made the mistake on a manuscript early in my career of frequently suggesting that an author "clarify" his writing. When I was cleaning up the manuscript after the author had responded to queries, I found a scrawled answer to my guidance several pages in. Where I had written "clarify" (using pencil on a Post-it back then), he had written, "READ!!!" His aggravation was obvious. I realized immediately that the writing *was* clear to the author, and my insensitive scribbling had only frustrated him and caused him to lose faith in me. What I needed to do was to suggest a couple of possible interpretations so he could see why I was confused. Fortunately, the senior editor who had hired me agreed that the writing lacked clarity and was willing to work with me to help me improve despite the author's irritation. Not all clients will do that. Some will lose patience and send the next manuscript to a different editor.

In another situation, I received a manuscript from a managing editor who told me that the author had been unhappy with a previous editor and wanted someone

Keep in Mind

"Maintaining a good relationship with the client is as important, if not more important, than the hands-on work I do."—Brian Jones, Freelance Editor new. Whenever you hear that an author or another client has been unhappy with an editor, it's a good idea to ask why. In this case, I learned that the original editor had told the author that he demonstrated a bias against Native Americans, a conclusion drawn after the editor had reviewed only the beginning pages of the manuscript and found several negative portrayals of Native Americans there. As it turned out, the author was Native American himself and was offended by the editor's judgment. Later chapters did include many positive portrayals of Native Americans, in fact, and balanced the book nicely. But instead of suggesting that readers might get a better overview if the early part of the book could be more balanced—and/or reading far enough to get a full perspective—the editor had judged the author's character and thereby destroyed all possibility of working with him. The author demanded that the publisher find a new editor.

Editors who offend authors will find little repeat work from their clients. Those who bring out the best from authors and keep them feeling positive about the publishing experience will be in demand.

Making Choices to Meet the Schedule and the Budget

No matter how brilliant you are as an editor, if you can't serve your client within the stated limitations, you won't be invited back. In chapter 5, "Managing Finances," we discussed things you could do to adjust an estimate if it was too high. One possibility was to discuss options for bringing the cost down. To reduce your time required, you might

- ask the client to do more tasks in-house: eliminate extra spaces in a manuscript, clean up formatting to make your work go more quickly, etc.;
- suggest that the client send some tasks back to the author: e.g., double-check scientific names of plant species or provide metric conversions;
- suggest to a scholarly client that a research assistant do more fact checking (you could point out examples of errors you have found and even provide a checklist of issues for the assistant to review); and/or
- find out if you can let go of some tasks—e.g., cleaning up passives.

Make it clear that you want to meet the client's budget or scheduling needs and are willing to compromise to do so. Then, if you agree to a budget, adhere to it. Ignoring your agreement will destroy the client's trust in you for future projects.

Being Flexible (to a Point)

As a freelancer, you are the client's hope for getting a job done on time. Unfortunately, clients sometimes seem to forget that home-based editors often work full-time, even though they might work only occasionally and part-time for any individual client. If an author gets a manuscript to the publisher late and the publisher in turn gets the manuscript late to you, then you might expect to have your deadline extended as well. That doesn't always happen, though. Furthermore, even if the deadline is extended, the new timeframe might not work for you. Instead of having job A from client A for the first two weeks of June and job B from client B for the last two weeks, for example, both jobs A and B might appear on your desk at the same time, with the same two-week turn-around. Client B probably doesn't know anything about client A—and job A is not client B's concern anyway. So now what do you do?

You might reasonably expect to tell client A that he's going to need to wait for an opening in your schedule. The problem is that client A might not be able to wait; his final deadline might be firm, regardless of slips early in the project. So then you might simply send the job back to client A, leaving him to deal with the problem.

But *now* the problem is that you were left sitting for two weeks earlier in the month waiting for project A without earning any pay. In fact, you *need* that job, no matter who was at fault for the disrupted schedule, in order to pay your bills.

Beyond that, even if the author for project A was the original problem, the client will likely be grateful for your help in averting the crisis. Juggling your schedule to accommodate the extra work might come back to you later when the client remembers how dependable you have been, hires you for the next job, and shares his good impressions with his colleagues who also hire freelancers. If you leave the job undone, that same client might forget the circumstances and recall later only that you left him with a problem. In other words, adjusting your personal life and working long hours for a time—even when the problem was not your doing—might later result in more work for you.

This kind of flexibility can be dangerous if a client learns to take advantage of you, however. How much you want to accommodate depends on how well established you are. Eventually, you might have all the work you need, and a couple of down weeks when something falls through might be acceptable or even welcome, especially if you could fill the time with nonurgent business (perhaps working on a new website or researching a potential new client). Or you might have enough work, and be enough in demand, that you can give up clients who repeatedly fail to meet their own deadlines. You will need to weigh the advantages against disadvantages. In short, though, the more accommodating you can be, the more likely your services will be in demand.

Following Up

After you have completed and sent off a job, make sure the client has received it. If you sent it on schedule and did not receive confirmation of its receipt, send a follow-up message or call the client to make sure the job arrived and ask if everything was clear. Again, don't take a lot of your client's time with long conversations, but express concern and interest in completing the job. If you enjoyed the work, mention that, and say that you would be happy to work on another project if the client has one that might be right for you. If you don't get another job, you could check back in later (maybe a few months later). Remind the client that you enjoyed doing the first job and ask if you might help with anything else. Keep the reminder concise so as not to be annoying.

> **Lessons Learned**
>
> "There's a lot of advice out there about networking, marketing, and pitching new clients, but none of those things will get you far unless you do quality work and deliver it on schedule. Marketing may get you new clients, but great work is what gets you repeat clients and referrals—the best way to sustain a business."—Juliet Clark, Freelance Editor

Resolving Problems

Occasionally you might hear from a client who is for some reason unhappy with your work. If this happens, and if the schedule allows, ask for details and request an opportunity to correct the problem. Remain professional. After you see the manuscript and hear more about the problem, if you feel responsible, apologize briefly and offer to redo the work without pay. If you feel that you were not responsible for the problem—maybe a time restriction prevented you from doing the level of work desired, or maybe the work was outside of your scope—explain calmly and succinctly without attacking or belittling the client in any way. Then offer to try to resolve the problem if you are able but plan to bill for your time.

It's important to defend your reputation but also to maintain goodwill. Keep in mind that your goal is to help the client produce a high-quality publication, and you need to work with (not against) the client. Regardless of fault, your professionalism in handling the situation will leave an impression and could affect your reputation for future work.

Working with Independent Authors

As self-publishing has become increasingly common, independent authors are more and more often direct clients, without a publisher in the middle. Projects for these independent authors can be some of the most rewarding of all. Some authors have researched the business of publishing and editing and have a good idea of what they want when they look for an editor. Some don't know what they want but trust a professional to lead them through the process.

Other independent authors, unfortunately, fail to understand what an editor can and cannot do but also lack respect for the editor as a professional. Because they are less familiar with the publishing process and less experienced in working with editors than other types of clients, they might have unrealistic expectations. Occasionally, no matter how good you are, you might find that you need to end a working relationship before a project is complete. In this case, it is important to recognize signs of trouble and cut your losses early on.

Some editors prefer to work directly with authors. They enjoy both the satisfaction and the challenge of helping the author. These editors especially have learned to communicate clearly and to take precautions. Following are some potential problems to watch for.

The Discreet Pleasures of Working with Individual Clients

San Francisco–based editor Christopher Bernard particularly enjoys working with independent authors on creative projects. Christopher, a published author himself, frequently helps his clients with development. He explains the satisfaction he gets this way:

"I often enjoy working with individual authors largely because, as a writer, I can usually sympathize with what they are trying to accomplish. I have been in their shoes for much of my professional life, writing out of love, passion, and faith; sometimes this faith has borne fruit, sometimes not, but I admire the belief in themselves these authors must have to follow the daunting master one's muse can be. Thus I have a deeper emotional connection with them than the inevitably more impersonal connection I have with business clients: We are more or less on the same team, and often see the world in a similar way. We belong to the same tribe. . . . I feel more personally involved and responsible, and this strengthens and deepens my commitment to the success of 'my authors.' When they succeed, I feel more gratified than I do with many other clients.

"In some ways the strongest pleasure for me is the depth and complexity of the work, which engages me intellectually, and with a level of that personal responsibility I mentioned, that I usually must save for my own literary projects. I often enjoy a challenge, and my imagination, my ability to structure and organize, my empathy, my inventiveness, and the like are needed at a level rarely called for elsewhere; my entire literary and editorial arsenal is required, whereas in most other editorial situations I feel I am using only a fraction of my abilities. The work therefore never suffers from my chief complaint about [other types of editorial projects]: monotony and lack of intellectual challenge, to say nothing of lack of autonomy."

The Client without Cash

Make sure to discuss early on with independent authors all matters of finance, including the maximum likely cost for a project. Many authors are shocked to hear that an edit could cost hundreds of dollars, let alone thousands or tens of thousands. Often they hope that you, the editor, will be as impassioned about their project as they are. Some write as a hobby, and they fail to realize that editing is *not* a hobby for you. For a beginning editor, still in need of experience for a résumé, these novice authors with little money might provide opportunities. If you are more experienced, though, don't give in. Keep the discussion professional—but no, you cannot work for a share of anticipated royalties. And even if you accept a low rate, discuss potential total expense early on and be firm about payments.

Especially with independent authors, some editors insist on partial payment for a project in advance. Some ask for half of the estimated total, others for a third or for a fixed amount. Another option is to exchange edited manuscript for a check. Whatever you do, make sure you get paid something before the author has all of your work. If the client can't pay, back out of the project before you invest a lot of time—or postpone your work until the author's finances are set. Don't wait until you have completed the job to find out that the client has no money at all.

The Client without Boundaries

Again especially for independent authors, make sure you set your boundaries. You might want to say that you work only weekdays until 6:00 p.m., for example. Enthusiastic authors might work day and night, but you are a professional, and you do not. Furthermore, no, the author cannot appear on your doorstep, and you cannot chat at all hours.

For some clients, you might need to limit telephone consultations. Make sure you let the client know that time in consultation is work time to be charged. Authors sometimes forget that you are working anytime you are communicating with them. They might be less likely to consider you a friend if they remember they will be billed for your time.

Ironically, some of the least respectful author-clients I have known when it comes to boundaries have also been some of the highest paying. Their ability to pay respectfully should help them hire an experienced professional. It does not entitle them to a twenty-four-hour-a-day consultant/therapist/friend.

The Client without Ethics

Occasionally a potential client will ask you to edit something that makes you uncomfortable—maybe a school application, a job application, a thesis or dissertation, or some other document intended to show the writing ability of the author. If you don't feel comfortable taking a job, don't. At one time, for example, I received a request for editorial assistance from a student with an application to graduate school as an English major. I was not comfortable with the request and did not help. In many other situations, however, assisting students is legitimate work. Some universities or individual professors even encourage students to get editorial assistance. "Indeed, it would be very helpful if students with poor writing could do this since it reduces the burden on professors," says one professor from a major university. "This is particularly true of English language learners." For further discussion and to help determine your own lines in this regard, see chapter 10, "Sizing Up Legal and Ethical Issues."

In other situations, an author might present a manuscript that supports something you find offensive. For example, I was asked another time (by someone who knew nothing about me) to edit a project with a neo-Nazi message. Some editors view such publications strictly from an intellectual perspective. If you are less open, know your own limitations and avoid the work without expressing judgment of the author. Don't waste time with an argument.

Even if you turn down a project, be professional. You never know who knows whom. Cut your losses and back out of a job if you need to, but do so gracefully, saying simply that this isn't the right job for you but that you wish the client well. Then look to the next potential job.

The Client without Talent

On rare occasion when I have edited a book for a publisher, I have found the manuscript to be so poorly written that I have felt compelled to point out the low quality to the assigning editor. In those cases, the assigning editor has expressed surprise, taken the manuscript back, and asked the author to work more or put the project on hold.

With independent authors, the situation is more sensitive. If you get a manuscript that turns out to be much weaker than you thought when you agreed to take it, what can you do? You have options depending on the situation.

- Consider the purpose. If Grandpa intends to self-publish his memoirs for the kids, the manuscript doesn't need to be brilliant. You could probably improve it significantly—and adequately—even if you can't make it a literary masterpiece. If you decide that this isn't work you enjoy, try to be more selective about projects in the future . . . but remember that Grandpa is counting on you, and carry through on your agreement to complete his project if you possibly can.
- If you really don't feel comfortable taking the client's money, state that you don't think you are the right editor for the project and back out. Try to do this early in the process so the client does not feel abandoned. Suggest to the author that she join a writers' group, where she could get general feedback without expense. Say that you aren't sure the manuscript is ready for an edit.

Some authors are determined to forge ahead. If that's the case, and if you have warned the author of your limitations, decide if you would like to take the job despite the flaws.

Be honest with the client without being brutal. Remember that a manuscript is very personal. For more on this issue, see chapter 10, "Sizing Up Legal and Ethical Issues."

The Client without Computer Skills

Even more so than other types of clients, independent authors sometimes lack computer skills commonly taken for granted in the business world today, particularly if the author grew up before computers were household items. A manuscript submitted singled-spaced and with narrow margins probably won't be a big problem; most editors can simply change the formatting to something more suitable. Even a manuscript with double spaces after every sentence, common practice from typewriter days, can easily be cleaned up with search and replace. But a client who has produced an entire manuscript using one of the basic word-processing programs that come installed on many computers could require a lot of time that has nothing to do with editing. Such manuscripts might not open easily in Word or another standard program. A client who has used primitive practices such as hitting the space bar multiple times instead of the tab key might also create extra work for the editor.

If you feel confident of your own computer skills, you can offer to help a computer-illiterate client put a manuscript into a more editable format. If you are unsure of your technical abilities beyond the basics, though, tell the client early on that she will need to find someone to convert the manuscript to Word or another format before you begin work. Let her know what you can and cannot do, and don't waste time struggling; I've seen freelance editors spend days trying to work with a file that should have been converted into a more workable program to begin with. In fact, you might want to insist that clients send you manuscripts in a particular format (probably Word). Editors who can help less computer-literate clients will have more opportunities, but speak up if you are not (or do not want to be) that kind of editor.

The Disillusioned Client

Every now and then a client might approach you for assistance but mention early in discussions that she had a previous editor who took a lot of her money but did poor work. Most likely this will be an independent author.

The problem? Editors do not require certification. You do not need to pass a test or earn a specific degree to work as an editor; you simply need to say you are an editor and convince someone to hire you. Most publishers and established businesses have some way to screen and assess freelancers before hiring them, but individuals are less systematic in their hiring decisions. Sadly, many hire based solely on an hourly rate, sometimes selecting the least experienced and least qualified person. Even more sadly, some pay respectable rates but are fooled by a good sales pitch that misleads them about the editor's ability.

If an author expresses concern based on a bad experience, try to find out why the client was unhappy. If possible, look at some sample work from the previous editor. Then try to determine what went wrong.

1. The author really did get a bad deal. In this case, you will want to do your best to demonstrate your superior ability and redeem the reputation of your profession.
2. The editor did a decent job but not the type of editing the client wanted. In this case, you will need to communicate carefully to make sure you are qualified to do a better job—and then do it.
3. The editor did exactly what you would do. In this case, you should back out of the job.

Some authors have unrealistic expectations. Some think they want help but have egos too large for them to accept the help when they get it. If this seems to be the situation, back out of a project early. Don't make assumptions, though. Sadly, just as some clients are disagreeable, some editors are unprofessional and/or unskilled. If your client has legitimate reason for concern, take the challenge to do better than the person before you.

The Positive Author-Client Experience

Despite the potential problems with independent authors, some of these authors make the best possible clients. Often independent authors are open to suggestions and respectful of an editor's professionalism. They are passionate about their work and excited about the help you give. Some can be less restrictive in requests than other clients; they might provide opportunities for an editor to combine development and copyediting skills, for example, or to do some production work and grapple with marketing issues as well as edit. If you enjoy playing a comprehensive role, this could appeal to you. In addition, because the client is the author, the editor needs to satisfy only one person and not a whole group of individuals involved in the publication. With the right fit, this work can be the most rewarding of all.

10

Sizing Up Legal and Ethical Issues

How Do You Protect Yourself and Your Client?

If you are reading this book, it's probably because you have chosen to be a home-based editor rather than to work as an employee. For the reasons discussed in chapter 1, "Making the Decision," you might prefer this setup to the structure of an employer-employee relationship. Sometimes, however, self-employed editors find themselves in situations where they seem to have all the disadvantages of employment but none of the benefits. You could find yourself committed to work for a single client full-time for months on end, required to work on-site. You might at first be excited about a stable job with a dream client and not even notice for a while that your contribution has evolved to mirror the contributions of employees getting full benefits. You might be perfectly happy working as a freelancer, in fact, even in this situation. You might like the stability of working long hours for a single client—but still with the freedom to take vacation with relatively little constraint.

Some clients, such as traditional publishers, hire freelancers with the required skills to do work as needed but do not require assistance from these workers on a regular basis. By hiring freelancers, these clients get the work done when needed without providing workspace, salary, and benefits for employees during slow times. In these situations, there is little doubt about the status of the contract editor.

But other companies need work done on an ongoing basis. So why wouldn't they hire employees? A company could be uncertain about the long-term need for help and reluctant to commit to hiring an employee. Or it could simply be trying to minimize costs. All of those employee benefits discussed in chapter 1 are expensive, and a company can save a great deal if it does not need to pay the employer's share of Social Security and Medicare, pay medical insurance, compensate for time off for vacation or illness, or contribute to a pension plan for the editor.

In some situations in the past, employers have been found to use freelance help unfairly to their benefit. Whether you are happy with your particular setup or not, the government requires that workers meet certain criteria to be considered freelancers. In one famous case, the IRS audited Microsoft and determined that many of the individuals hired as part of the company's "contingent workforce" (contract help) for open tax years 1989 and 1990 had actually provided the same services to Microsoft as employees had. Freelancers had been working alongside employees at the company, performing identical functions under like conditions but without receiving benefits. Despite the fact that the individuals—including production editors, proofreaders, indexers, and others—had signed agreements with Microsoft regarding their freelance status, the IRS eventually determined that they were de facto employees. At least for tax purposes, they were not independent contractors. Among the determining factors: The contractors worked on-site, often on teams with employees; shared the same supervisors and performed the same functions as employees; used the same office equipment and supplies; and held the same hours.

In more recent years, clients have been careful to distinguish between employees and freelancers: Big corporate clients don't want the IRS challenging them any more than independent freelancers do. The IRS has developed guidelines to help define freelancers and to protect workers who might be deprived of their rights by greedy corporations. For the responsible client and the freelancer who truly wants to freelance, precautions—often involving paperwork and freelancer burden of proof to establish status—can be annoying. But they are intended to protect both client and freelancer and usually require only that the freelancer and the hiring manager answer some basic questions.

Defining Yourself as a Freelancer

According to the IRS, "The general rule is that an individual is an independent contractor if the payer has the right to control or direct only the result of the work and not what will be done and how it will be done."[1] Editors who have a variety of small

---

1 Internal Revenue Service, "Independent Contractor Defined," www.irs.gov/Businesses/Small-Businesses-&-Self-Employed/Independent-Contractor-Defined, accessed December 17, 2012.

Factors Commonly Considered in Determining Freelance Status

Following are just some of the issues companies consider to determine whether a worker is an employee or an independent contractor, based on IRS guidelines. The IRS lists twenty issues of importance overall. Those discussed here are often considered particularly relevant for home-based editors. A freelancer does not need to answer all questions in a specific way; status is determined by the combination of answers.

Instructions. Freelancers typically receive fewer specific instructions from clients than employees do. Freelancers determine their own means of accomplishing the required work.

Training. Freelancers rarely receive specific training for a job. They are expected to have the required skills.

Continuing relationship. An employee who leaves a staff position but continues to do the same work for a substantial amount of time is probably still an employee. One who provides services infrequently as needed is probably a freelancer.

Set hours of work. Freelancers typically set their own hours.

Full-time requirement. Freelancers typically have discretionary hours and are rarely required to work full-time for a single client for an extended period of time.

Work performed at the employer's place of business. Employees are more likely to work at a client's site regularly for an extended period of time. Freelancers also work on-site at times but rarely regularly. Note, though, that many employees now telecommute, so work from a home office alone does not necessarily establish freelance status.

Responsibility for business and travel expenses. Freelancers typically absorb travel expenses as part of an independent business.

Provision of tools and materials. Freelancers typically use their own equipment and supplies to perform a task. In addition, freelancers often own major equipment needed to do a job, such as computer equipment and other resources.

Work for more than one client at a time. Most freelancers have multiple clients. Employees are more likely to work exclusively for one client. Variety in clientele is one of the most important ways for a freelancer to establish independence.

Services available to the general public. Freelancers market their services to the public. Proof of advertising is a good way to establish freelance business.

jobs for many clients probably don't need to worry about proving freelance status. Those who work primarily for a single client might need to be more concerned about the work relationship, even if they do most or all of the work from a home office. In some cases, the employer requires a potential freelancer to complete a questionnaire to determine worker relationship and protect the client from potential lawsuits. Different clients use different combinations of questions (see "Factors Commonly Considered in Determining Freelance Status," page 167, for descriptions of issues often addressed for editors).

To protect themselves, some large clients now hire freelancers only through agencies or other businesses that will verify the independent status of the workers. Editors who want to work for these businesses, often technical corporations, might need to connect with an agency, or approved vendor, in order to get that work. The agency serves to protect both the freelancer and the hiring company and often handles tax issues. Sometimes contractors work as temporary employees in this situation rather than as freelancers. Freelancers should make sure they understand expenses associated with working through the agency—primarily a fee or a commission on work performed in this way. A home-based editor who wants to work for a client that insists on this type of setup should value the service of the agency but must understand fees and tax issues when considering the arrangement.

Considering Contracts

For one-time jobs with publishers, other small businesses, or independent authors, editors are rarely asked to sign contracts. To work with larger businesses, even if the job is relatively small, however, you might need to sign a formal contract. This is often true for technical companies, health care organizations, and university departments, for example.

Some editors sign contracts without reading them thoroughly and never regret doing so. When I am asked to sign a contract, though, I read the pages word for word. Often a legal department within a large company has generated the contract, and the company attempts to use the same contract for all freelancers. Often these contracts have clauses in them that do not reasonably apply to editors. Again, some editors overlook these clauses and trust that all will be well. I do not. Some clients argue that the words really don't mean that much and might pressure you to sign quickly to move forward with a job. I would not do this.

Some clauses are particularly important for editors. Always pay attention to the following, for example.

Nondisclosure Agreements

Companies often ask editors not to share the content of the documents being edited, often until the work is published and sometimes indefinitely. It is important to note and comply with this clause when you accept a job. If you have signed a nondisclosure agreement (NDA) for a company, you cannot discuss the content of any work with others or show a sample of your work to another client without expressed permission. Potential clients often ask to see samples of work, so make note of any sample that cannot be shared and honor the agreement you have signed.

Insurance Requirements

Boilerplate contracts often have extensive requirements in terms of insurance. I have seen contracts that required editors to have, for example,

- $2 million in liability insurance
- $1 million in workers' compensation insurance
- $1 million in automobile insurance

Some of this insurance is reasonable for editors to have. Liability insurance might be a good idea, for example, depending on the type of work you do. See chapter 4, "Getting Started," for a discussion of this type of insurance.

Other insurance requirements make little sense for a freelance editor. As a sole proprietor without employees, you probably do not need workers' compensation insurance, for example (although laws vary by place and time). And if you work from a home office, with a ten-step commute from your kitchen to your desk, you do not need $1 million in automobile insurance. You might not need any automobile insurance at all.

In recent years, many clients have realized the absurdity of asking a freelance editor to meet such requirements. Contracts that have crossed my desk lately have had language such as, "Contractor will have insurance as required by law." This vague provision allows you to sign the contract without discussion.

If more specific language remains and you feel uncomfortable with the conditions, talk to the client. Often you can simply cross out or delete the unreasonable requirement. More rarely, a client insists that the contract cannot be altered. In that case, you need to decide whether to enlist the help of your own lawyer to negotiate.

Sometimes the job is large enough that it's worth investing time and money to comply with client requirements—and compliance might be less expensive than a battle. If you find yourself in this situation, start with a call to your insurance agent. You might be able to get "combined single limit" coverage to satisfy your client—or you might get by with general liability insurance alone. As an example of such a situation, I acquired business insurance myself years ago when a prize client required I have it. Although I didn't understand the requirement at the time, the work I got from the client then and for years afterward more than justified the investment. I paid under $200 a year for the insurance and got thousands of dollars worth of interesting work over many years.

At other times, you might decide a job is not worth the effort or expense of obtaining additional insurance and choose instead to look for another job.

Exclusivity

Contracts sometimes specify that you may not work for any competitor of the company. Take note of such clauses, and determine whether the condition is acceptable given the nature of your work. In some cases, you might already work for a competitor. If this creates a problem for you, talk to the client. Again, clients are sometimes willing to cross out the clause.

Terms of Work

Always check payment terms: hourly or project rate, maximum amount allowable for work performed, schedule, and so on. These details are sometimes in the body of the contract and sometimes in an addendum or exhibit.

Terms of Payment

Also check terms of payment to make sure they are agreeable. Contracts often give clear details about where, when, and how to submit invoices (via e-mail? snail mail?) as well as when the payment will be processed. If a contract states that payment will be made sixty days after receipt of the invoice, for example, ask your contact if that time can be reduced to thirty days. Your contact might not have any control over the terms, but you can ask. If the client can't budge and you won't either, you might need to give up the job. Just make sure you understand the terms at the outset if you accept the work so you can manage your budget appropriately.

Working without a Contract

Most freelancers skip the contract if the client doesn't require it. In more than twenty years of freelancing, I have never been asked by a book publisher to sign a formal contract. In fact, you might annoy a managing editor if you insist on a formal contract to do a routine job. It's always important to make sure you and your client have a clear agreement about what you will do, however, and it's easy enough to put this in writing, send it in an e-mail, and ask your client to acknowledge receipt and let you know if your understanding is accurate. You might say, for example, "As I understand it, we have agreed to the following. . . . Please let me know if this is your understanding as well."

In your agreement, be sure to specify the following:

- The job assignment. Include the project title and word count if you have one or some other indication of how much work will be involved.
- The service. Will you be proofreading? Light-level copyediting? Heavy-level copyediting? Something else?
- Number of passes. Will you do one pass? Two? Will you handle clean-up?
- The rate. Include your billing unit (hour, page, project) and rate per unit.
- An estimate of the total expected. Give a range with a cap, if possible.
- Assumptions. If you give a cap, state that you will honor the cap assuming certain things—for example, that the sample material you received was representative, that you will receive Word documents in a standard format, that the manuscript will be a certain length, and so on.
- The schedule. State the deadline and any interim deadlines (for example, four chapters to be returned at a certain time, first pass to be completed by a given date, etc.). Again, indicate that you promise to meet your schedule only if you receive materials from the client at the time promised.

- For independent authors, boundaries to be respected. You will be available for business communications weekdays 8:00 a.m. to 5:00 p.m., for example. While traditional publishers might have their own boundaries, individual authors often work on personal projects during odd hours themselves and sometimes expect editors to be available for consultation seven days a week twenty-four hours a day. If you are willing to answer questions on weekends or evenings, that's your choice. If not, make clear when you do work.

For an example of an informal letter of agreement—something between the many pages of legalese provided by large companies and the informal e-mail suggested here—see page 173.

Calming the Concerned Client

Authors working independently sometimes express concern that an editor might lift their material for personal benefit. If a potential client questions you about this, assure the author that you could not stay in business if you didn't respect an author's rights. Point out that an author automatically owns the rights to any original words as soon as they are put on paper. You could suggest that a concerned author print "Copyright © [name]" at the bottom of all pages, even in manuscript form, to remind readers—including the editor—that the author is attentive to the issue. And note that registration with the US Copyright Office upon publication provides extra support in case of dispute. But again, none of this is necessary to determine copyright ownership; authors have all rights to their own work until they sign away those rights.

If you are like me and many other editors I talk with, you might smile at the author's belief that the work presented is so original and so good that you would steal it. But hide your smile; realize that the concern is reasonable even if it's probably unnecessary. Such things have happened in the past, and the issue is serious for an author.

Pondering Ethical Issues

As new editors, especially if we are nervous about paying our bills, many of us are tempted to accept any job that comes our way. Before accepting work, though, make sure you are qualified to do the work and will feel good about taking pay for it. Following are just a few things to consider before you agree to do a job.

Barbara Fuller

My Address

My Phone

My E-mail

December 3, 2053

Dear Ms. Publisher:

This letter confirms my agreement with **Hound Publishing, Inc.,** to provide copyediting services for the book **How to Raise a Dog, by John Beagle,** on the following terms and conditions:

Service to be provided: medium-level copyediting

Fee: $30 per hour for 36 to 44 hours of work, or $1,080 to $1,320 total (actual hours to be billed)

Expenses to be reimbursed in addition to the fees listed above: None

Schedule:

- Manuscript received for copyedit: January 3, 2053

- Copyedited manuscript returned to publisher: January 17, 2053

- Manuscript returned to copyeditor with answers to queries for clean-up: January 31, 2053

- Manuscript cleaned up and returned to publisher: February 7, 2053

I will complete my work as indicated above, provided I receive a manuscript of approximately 65,000 words on schedule as noted. If delays are caused by anyone or anything other than myself, the schedule for remaining work is subject to renegotiation.

I will bill as follows:

- For original copyediting: Hours worked to be billed January 17

- For clean-up: Hours worked to be billed February 7

- All invoices will be itemized and will be due and payable within thirty days of receipt.

I acknowledge that my services as described herein constitute work for hire, and I disclaim all rights to copyright with respect to any work that is deliverable under this agreement. However, I will receive two (2) copies of the finished work, which I may freely use for portfolio presentation or other self-promotion, or by photocopying portions of the work for the same purposes.

I am an independent contractor, and I am responsible for the supervision, management, and control of the means of fulfilling my duties. I am not an employee of **Hound Publishing, Inc.**

Continued on next page

This shall constitute the entire agreement between us, may be modified only in writing, and shall be governed by California state law.

Each of the undersigned has the authority to make this a binding agreement.

If these terms are agreeable to you, please sign below to indicate your acceptance and return this letter to me. A copy is enclosed for your files.

Agreed to:

_____

Barbara Fuller   Title   Date

_____

Name   Title   Date
Hound Publishing, Inc.

Determining Your Qualifications

Always ask yourself if you have the skills required to do a job well. If not, are you close—and are you willing and able to do what is necessary to acquire the skills you lack? If you are a strong editor and have worked in health care, for example, would you be a good medical editor for a journal? If you have the appropriate resources, you might be. But if you don't do the job well, you could be letting your client down, and word could travel.

If you are a bit shy of experience, you might consider some of the time you spend as learning time and not as billable work. Are you looking up too many words in a medical dictionary because even some of the most common medical jargon is unfamiliar to you? Maybe you should stop the clock for a time.

When I began copyediting, I realized that my lack of experience meant I needed to check things in my *Chicago Manual of Style* that a more experienced editor would have known. I also knew that I needed my clients to be happy if I wanted continuing assignments; I was determined to turn in manuscripts that were error-free. (I was naïve enough in my early years to think that was always possible.)

For many assignments in the beginning, I would read the manuscript one more time than expected at no charge to the client. After I built a little experience, I stopped doing this in general—but I still occasionally make an extra free pass if I am working in new territory. I did this the first time I edited a cookbook, for example, even though I had years of editing experience behind me by then. I knew I was making decisions slowly and sometimes changing my mind about things because I lacked experience with cookbooks in particular. And while an employee would be paid for training on the job, clients expect freelancers to be experts already. (The situation might be different if an existing client asks you to do a job that is beyond your usual reach. In that case, you might explain that you will need extra time to get up to speed and expect to be paid for that time.)

In general, I do not advocate underbilling; it's important for a client to know how much time a job actually takes. But again, I considered this extra pass to be self-education.

Dealing with Disagreeable Content

A good editor needs to be able to maintain an objective eye. If you have strong opinions about something that might make it difficult for you to be objective, it's important to realize that. This might apply particularly to political or religious content or perhaps to alternative health issues. I know many fine editors who can work on any content and keep an even eye. If you don't feel that you can do that, though, know when a subject is not right for you, and turn down the job. You are not hired to coach an author about what to think or a publisher about what to publish. You are hired to help the author communicate clearly whatever the author intends to communicate.

Drawing the Line: Student Work and Applications

Increasingly, students working on dissertations and theses are asking editors to help them with their final work. Some editors, in fact, specialize in working with these students. Often students seek help because

- some universities routinely ask students to have master's theses proofread before they are bound,
- some professors or committees accept PhD dissertations but then advise students to have the dissertation copyedited before it is bound,
- some students speak English as a second language and need assistance articulating clearly in writing, and

■ some students simply want to submit the best possible work they can and seek professional help on their own.

As a rule, it's a good idea to ask students who contact you whether a lead professor or committee knows they are seeking outside assistance. Typically, the committee has suggested that the student get help; many universities advise students to check in at a campus writing center or to hire an approved proofreader before submitting a thesis or dissertation. Others advise students to find their own editor or proofreader.

Some professors object to such practices, however, and expect their students to submit work without assistance. One way to avoid overstepping in these cases is to ask your client to tell her professor that she is getting help. Use your judgment in accepting work, avoid crossing the line between editing and writing, and keep records of what you have done and suggested (with tracked changes or memos to the student) in case questions arise.

Related to the issue of assisting students with their work of scholarship is the issue of assisting potential clients with applications for graduate school or employment. In determining whether to accept such work, consider the applicant's goal. If the application is to demonstrate an individual's ability to write—as with an essay presented for a grad school application—I would be wary of assisting beyond proofreading. If the applicant is applying for a job that does not require writing skills and simply wants to ensure a clean presentation of ideas, I would be inclined to help more.

Letting Go: Knowing When You Can't Help

Occasionally you will realize soon after starting a project that the author *can't write*. It's not just that you dislike the author's style or lack interest in the subject matter; you know that the words on your screen will never merit professional publication and that even self-publication could embarrass the author. As an editor who has reserved time to work on the book and has bills looming, do you continue? Is it your place to tell the author?

Occasionally this happens when a publisher has accepted a proposal and is not aware that the manuscript submitted is weak. In this situation, explain your concern and point to specific examples of problems. If you have ideas for moving ahead— hire another writer to revise the manuscript or a developmental editor to rework it, for example—suggest them to the publisher. Then ask the publisher to advise you regarding next steps. If you keep working, turn in a hopeless manuscript, and submit a bill, the client might lose faith in you and your judgment.

More often such poorly written manuscripts come from independent authors who hope to find a publisher. In such a case, if you are considering working with the client despite your lack of confidence in the work, make sure the author understands that you cannot promise a sale; you are not an agent or an expert in marketing. You might say that you doubt whether the manuscript will be marketable even with a careful edit. Keep the criticism focused on the project and not on the author. Say that you know that your work is expensive. If the client assures you that he knows there are no guarantees and insists that he wants you to do the job anyway, decide whether to move ahead or not. Sometimes an individual author wants to learn from the process. Sometimes he is determined to self-publish if he can't find a traditional publisher—and you can probably help him improve the work even if it remains weak. Just make clear that you can't promise a publishable manuscript and, if appropriate, that you think success will be unlikely. Back out if you think you should, perhaps suggesting that the author join a writers' group to get feedback at no cost.

How Much Do You Bill? Honesty in Billing

As a home-based editor, you will probably be responsible for tracking, reporting, and billing for hours worked on a project. Editors who work strictly on a project or milestone basis avoid this requirement, but as we have discussed, many prefer to bill by the hour.

I once attended a discussion among editors with a now-defunct organization where a lead speaker asked if anyone ever overbilled. I was surprised to hear that many did, although some had strange ways to justify what they did. One claimed to bill honestly but said she considered fifty minutes to be an hour (because no employee would actually concentrate for a full hour without pause); another said he gave himself a half-hour paid break for every four hours of work. I asked editors in my own group the same question and learned that they were more likely to underbill than to overbill; they were more concerned about appearing to work too slowly than about being paid too little. Although clients would probably prefer the model of underbilling, the potential problems are great in this case for freelancers who later work with clients who have unrealistic expectations.

If you overbill, you are cheating the client. If you underbill, you are misrepresenting the freelancer. A client can understand the time required to do a good job only if you bill honestly. A modification might occasionally be justified—if you believe you spent part of your time teaching yourself skills that the client might reasonably have expected you to have already, for example. But if you want to help a nonprofit because you like what the client is doing and know it can't pay, offer the client a special low project rate (and let the client know what you are doing). Don't pretend that the job was easier than it was; doing so will make the work impossible for the next freelancer who comes along.

If you know that you work much slower or much faster than most editors do, consider requesting a project rate. If you are slow but are willing to put in the extra time needed, the client will get the work done for a fixed rate without needing to worry about hours. And if you work more efficiently than most, a project rate could result in the higher hourly rate you think you deserve (and probably do if you are really that fast). In both situations, the client presumably pays a fair rate without any manipulation of hours.

11

Balancing Business and Family

How Do You Draw Lines and Make Sure That Others Respect Them?

Having a career that you can operate from your home often seems like a win-win situation for a parent on a career path but also committed to raising a family. Moms and dads alike have long attempted to maximize their time with their children and be successful in two different worlds.

But balancing a career and a family under the same roof can be more difficult than it might seem, especially if you are attempting to work full-time. Work-at-home parents sometimes come to feel that they are shortchanging both their business and their family. The setup works well for many parents, but it's not for everyone, and it's important to have realistic expectations.

This chapter is intended for parents who work at home, particularly for those attempting to work full-time. Some of the material will be relevant for individuals who are responsible for other dependents or who split their work time with other demanding responsibilities. Those with fewer conflicts should skip to chapter 12.

Combining Parenthood with Work at Home: The Pros

If you are deciding whether to begin a freelance career with the idea that working from home will make you a better parent, consider first both the potential advantages and the potential disadvantages of such a work situation. Many of us start out full of idealism as we anticipate the advantages.

- As a home-based editor, you will be close to your family, under the same roof with your children when they are not in school or elsewhere.

- You can often work flexible hours, day or night, weekday or weekend, scheduled around the lives of your children.
- You can stop work to attend school functions, chaperone field trips, or help in a child's classroom.
- You can adjust your schedule to transport a child to music lessons, school clubs, and other extracurricular activities.
- You can volunteer to help with sports, Scouts, or other activities of interest to you and your child.
- When your children are home from school, you can have lunch with them rather than with colleagues who might be less important to you.
- You can be at home with a sick child without having to make special arrangements to miss a day of work. As a work-at-home parent, you can put your sick child to bed, check on her occasionally, and continue to work—a benefit to your child and to your child's school, which all too often has children attending when they are unwell but have nowhere else to go.
- You might be able to give yourself a vacation to coincide with your children's vacation. You might have more weeks off than if you were employed.
- Without a commute, you will probably save time and can give that time to either your business or your family.
- You might save money by reducing or eliminating the need for child care.
- For women, you can breastfeed an infant longer and more easily than if you work in an office away from the home.

Combining Parenthood with Work at Home: The Cons

As in other areas, it is easy to glamorize the expected lifestyle of a work-at-home parent and neglect to consider the downsides. Some of the disadvantages of working at home as a parent can be foreseen. Others are less obvious at first or depend on individual situations. Following are some of the disadvantages you might expect.

- You will have your work with you at all times, twenty-four hours a day, seven days a week. You might find it difficult to set your work completely aside for your family.
- Likewise, you might find it difficult to say no to your family when you have work to do.

- You might feel isolated when you focus on work but have no colleagues nearby.
- Unless you hire assistance, you will have no one to depend on for help when you need it. If you do not have outside child care, you will be responsible for your children even when you have work to do—and you will be responsible for your work even when you have children to parent.
- You might find yourself easily distracted from your work. If you are a procrastinator, you could have difficulty staying focused with so many personal priorities imminent.
- Friends and family members might consider you to be available for personal time whenever they want you to be and find it difficult to respect your work time.
- You might find it difficult to say no to requests for help from people who consider you to be available. After all, you *could* shift your work schedule to help with one of the myriad tasks that stay-at-home parents help with.
- Friends with jobs away from home might begin asking you to help with their children, not realizing that you, too, are a working parent with other responsibilities.
- You might have difficulty shifting from personal life to work life to personal life and back. If you take an hour off to volunteer at your child's school, you could have difficulty getting back on task with your editing when you return home to work.

- You will lack the security of a fixed income and will need to budget carefully, as discussed in chapter 5, "Managing Finances."
- If you take a sick day—for yourself or for your child—you will not be paid. This is also true for maternity leave, unless you have purchased disability insurance independently.
- You might find yourself committed to your work even when your children have vacation time to spend with you.
- You will not have paid vacation, insurance benefits, or other employee benefits.

Setting Boundaries

The secret to success in blending personal and professional lives is in the lines—both spatial and temporal. Setting boundaries is key.

The Office

For everything there is a place—and anyone expecting to successfully run a business from home with children in it needs to know what space is what. I talked in chapter 3 about the home office and offered examples including separate rooms as well as designated parts of general rooms. When children are at home, it can be even more important than otherwise to separate and define a workspace. A parent with a desk in the corner of the living room will have difficulty concentrating on work. You will want a separate space where you can focus on your work when you need to, probably a space with a door that closes. Depending on the age of your children and other help in the house, you might even want a door with a lock.

If your children are old enough, explain to them that they may not disturb you when you are working except in cases of emergency. Then discuss "emergency." Hunger probably doesn't qualify. A squabble with a sibling probably doesn't, either.

Younger children will not understand boundaries; a rational explanation of your need for privacy won't mean a thing to a toddler who doesn't understand *work* or *privacy* but does understand that you are present and should be focused on *her*. One freelancer with young children had such a hard time getting her children to understand that she started a routine of leaving her house each morning with her husband and young children inside, walking around the block, and sneaking in the back door of her home and into her office without her children seeing her so they did not know she was there.

Keeping your office separate from your personal space could be necessary for financial reasons as well as for focus. Remember that you can deduct home office expenses when figuring your income tax, but only if you use an office exclusively for business. Also reserve your computer for your work if at all possible, even if it is portable. Not only could children create problems if they get into your files, but their very presence affects what you can write off as a business deduction. Again, keep the lines clear. Your computer is not a toy for them or even a tool for them to use when doing their schoolwork. It's part of your business, just as if it were sitting on a work desk in another town.

The Work Schedule

For everything there is also a time. Some work-at-home parents have clear schedules. They might work only mornings (while the children are at preschool, for example) and evenings (after a spouse arrives home). They might refuse to work after a certain hour (maybe 9:00 p.m.), or they might work *primarily* after a certain hour (an 8:00 p.m. bedtime, for example). Setting up such basic guidelines for yourself is a good idea. To take advantage of your work-at-home status, you will probably want to make exceptions at times, but find a balance that works for you.

Let your family know what your work times are. Although some clients might care vaguely about your children, most do not want to hear about the kids. They want even less to hear *from* the kids. Keep your talk professional, and do your best to find times to talk on the phone without high-pitched voices in the background.

Also let your clients know when you cannot work. It is far too easy to let your work crowd every minute of every day. It's important for your children to know at some point that they are first priority. If you can't make that happen, you might question whether your good intentions as a parent with a home office are really working out for you.

Advice from a Freelancer

"Maintain boundaries between your work life and your real life (e.g., don't answer the phone after 5:30, take days off, etc.)."—A Freelance Editor

Volunteerism

Under the list of advantages at the beginning of this chapter, I included three that have been particularly significant to me:

- You can stop work to attend school functions, chaperone field trips, or help in a child's classroom.
- You can adjust your schedule to transport a child to music lessons, school clubs, and other extracurricular activities.
- You can volunteer to help with sports, Scouts, or other activities of interest to you and your child.

But I also listed two disadvantages at the beginning of this chapter that have been particular problems for me:

- Friends and family might consider you to be available for personal time whenever they want you and find it difficult to respect your work time.
- You might find it difficult to say no to requests for help from people who consider you to be available.

For me, the second of these two points has probably been the bigger issue; the problem is in my own weakness when it comes to establishing boundaries. I have served as room parent, Girl Scout leader, band booster, soccer team mom, swim team mom, and board member for various school clubs over eighteen years now for my three children, with more years ahead. I do these things because I want to be a part of my children's lives—because I love my role as a parent just as much as I thrive on my career as an editor. But at times I have felt myself overextended, and while I have been careful not to short my clients, I have sometimes become short with my family.

Keep in Mind

There's a big difference between being a stay-at-home parent and being a work-at-home parent. The challenge to working at home is drawing lines where you need them.

None of us can do it all. For years, I worked long into the nights, sometimes turning out the light at 2:00 a.m. and setting the alarm for 6:00 a.m. Often I have worked weekends, hiding myself away when my husband, Kevin, was home to help with the kids. This can work in the short term—but not in the long. In addition to the physical wear, such overextension will eventually lead to inferior work. My approach now is to set the beginning of my day and the end, designate enough time for my work, designate at least some time for my family each day, and then determine whether I can give more and where.

Exploring Day-Care Options

The woman who walked around the block and hid in her office was not alone with her children; someone else was in the house. Younger children need the presence of an older person nearby, both physically and mentally. Although many of us begin a freelance career with the idea that we will avert the need for child care, many of us eventually rethink. While a child might self-entertain for a short period of time, depending on the age, you might need the help of a spouse, an extended family member, or a paid caregiver when you work. Or you might decide to send the children elsewhere, at least for a little while. No one would believe that leaving a child alone for hours on end is a good idea, even with an adult in the house.

How much help and what kind you need will depend on your individual child or children, the number of children you have, and other individuals involved. It will also depend on how much you need or want to work; those who work part-time might be able to balance things without outside assistance. Every family is different, but following are a few observations that I have made in raising my own three children, together with some input and suggestions from others.

Children in the First Year

Even if you make the decision to start a home-based business while expecting your first baby, as many people do, give yourself some time immediately after the birth. You might think you can keep working, but you would probably do better to take a break. Having a newborn at home is stressful, and you need to present your best business side when you approach clients.

If you are already working and have continuing clients, let them know about your expected infant. When my first child was born, I was fortunate enough to have a client who sent me small jobs on loose deadlines. I told him I expected a child in

June and could not take anything on a tight deadline for a month before that or for a couple of months afterward. I did not accept any larger projects.

Another editor and new mom I know thought she could continue work up until her child was born and start again soon after. But she found herself missing deadlines and had to back out on at least one project that she had promised to take, leaving her client without a plan. No matter how understanding a client might seem to be, clients depend on you to meet your deadlines—and failure to do so could destroy the client's trust in you. It's better to be honest about your lack of control over your schedule for a few months and to be dependable when you start work again.

After your baby is born, in the early months, you might be able to work with your infant nearby. Try working while he sleeps if possible, and don't overbook yourself. Remember that exhaustion from broken sleep will probably affect the quality of your work. You don't want to disappoint a client, who might seem to sympathize but really just needs a job done well. A client who loses faith in you might disappear and be uninterested in working with you again even after your life becomes more stable.

As your baby grows for the first half a year or so, he will sleep a lot, and he will be able to self-entertain some of the time in a confined space. If you can focus on your work, go ahead. This child will learn from a young age that work is part of your world—and of his. Talk to your baby between periods of concentration, and take advantage of nap time whenever possible. Also consider working when a spouse is home or when a member of your extended family can be in the home with you.

Over the next few months, your baby will become more mobile. He will begin to crawl and then to walk. By the time he reaches a year old, you will find yourself much less in control, increasingly unable to focus on your work with your baby in sight.

The Preschool Years

When my children were young, they were far too active to let me work, and I was unwilling to confine them or to set them in front of a television to give myself quiet time. The illusion of children without child care was dissolving. For me and my children, it seemed that "raising them myself" was not working, and letting them raise themselves was not in anyone's best interest.

I experimented with a variety of setups. I hadn't wanted day care at all in the beginning, but I soon realized that my children were getting less attention from me than they could get from a helper. At different times, I had the following:

- A young neighbor girl who played with my oldest child while I worked. Sophie was thirteen when she first came to our home, and she loved children. She would bring her own books and craft projects for my daughter Kristina, and at her young age, she was delighted with the little money I could give her in the beginning. Although she was younger than I might have liked for a babysitter alone with my toddler, I was comfortable having her in my living room while I worked in my office—and as it turned out, she was more attentive than some of the older sitters I later found. Sophie remained a special friend to Kristina and was a helper until she graduated from high school and moved away to college.
- A home day-care provider. When Kristina was a bit older and I needed more help with her, I took her to a woman who lived nearby. There my daughter interacted with four other young children three afternoons a week. By sending her for just this limited time, I ensured myself a minimum of solid work time, ensured my daughter some social time, and kept my costs low.
- A neighbor with another child my daughter's age. I could not exchange babysitting hours but paid my neighbor, a stay-at-home mom with a daughter the same age as Kristina. My second daughter, Alicia, had arrived by then, too, and my neighbor was happy to have playmates for her little girl. Alternatively, I know freelancers who have joined babysitting pools with friends, neighbors, or fellow church members. Freelancers with this arrangement have some concentrated work time and some good-quality time with their children and friends. The setup works especially well for someone with a part-time workload.
- A full-time home day care. By the time my third child was born, my girls were in school and I had a full-time business. But I had met a woman who had a home day-care business and was wonderful with children. Sonia cared for Anthony from the time he was two until he went to school—and occasionally on vacation days after that. I had absolute trust in her, and she had such a positive effect on my son that Anthony, now approaching middle school, still stops by to visit her on occasion. I never regretted leaving him with her, despite my original intent of keeping my young children close to me at all times.

Another option is a child-care center. Although I never chose this arrangement for my own children, some friends have had positive experiences leaving their children in centers. Many such centers also offer an educational curriculum that can benefit preschool children. If you explore this possibility, start by asking about hours; does the center offer part-time care to meet your needs? Do your research, and talk to others who leave their children in the center to find out what they like or dislike about it.

Early School Years

Once your children begin school, you will have built-in child-free times to work at home. Make sure you use those times well. Don't let yourself get distracted or stop to chitchat with other parents dropping off children at school. Yes, it would be nice to get the grocery shopping out of the way, but you need to do that later with the children in tow. You are not a stay-at-home mom or dad. You are a work-at-home mom or dad, and you need to get busy. You need to be disciplined—even more disciplined than the parent who drops a child off in the morning and then commutes to a distant office to punch a clock.

Depending on how much work you have and want, you might consider after-school care during these years as well. Again, needs and opportunities vary. I have gone through periods of time when I had my children home after school every day to entertain themselves. Sometimes and at some ages that works. But when I found my son sitting in front of the television for too many hours, I put him in an after-school program three afternoons a week where he could have social time and stimulation. The day-care staff helped him with his homework and then sent him off to play with other children, both indoors and out.

Older Children

As the kids grow older, they are better able to self-entertain and probably disciplined enough to do their own homework and take care of other responsibilities while you work. If they have grown up with you working at home, they will respect your space and need for quiet.

Although care of young children is the obvious concern for a work-at-home parent, however, spending a few minutes after school visiting with my older children has been perhaps one of the most rewarding aspects of working at home for me. Often by dinnertime, events of the day are far removed, and the things that bother or excite teens have slipped from their minds. Being able to sit down at the table for a snack when the kids first get home and chat for fifteen minutes or half an hour about their school day is invaluable. After that short time, I could return to my work and they to their homework.

Getting Other Help

If you are determined to keep your career on the fast track and also to give to your children as much as the parents who do not balance high-powered careers, think about other ways to get help.

Split Shifts of Parenting

I talked earlier about having a helper at the house while I was home. Some people designate work time when the spouse is home for "parent duty" (*not* "babysitting duty" when a parent is involved, as my husband will tell you adamantly). Consider your work-at-home time just as you might consider a swing shift outside the house; it's time when you are not available, and the other partner is in charge.

This type of arrangement can work well for the short term as you begin to build your business on a tight budget or when you have an occasional overload of work, when you just couldn't get everything done during your standard day. But attempting to split shifts with a spouse over long periods of time can be wearing. Don't lose sight of your personal needs in caring for your business and your children. If you have other options, explore them.

Help with Other Routine Activities

Depending on your financial situation, consider hiring assistance with routine tasks. If you can find the work to keep busy editing, free up your time for your job and let others do the jobs they love to do. Maybe you could hire a housekeeper or a gardener. There's nothing wrong with wanting to be both a career person and a good parent. For the short term, you might be able to work the long hours you need. But for the long term, figure out what you can give up, and give it up as soon as you are able. Do what you do well, and let others do what they do. You won't be able to do it all.

12 Developing and Expanding Your Business

What Do You Do Next?

Throughout this book, I have emphasized the freelancer's need to master strong business skills, including networking and marketing skills. This is not because business skills are more important than editorial skills. On the contrary: Business skills are secondary. Editorial talent should be first on your list of requirements for success. My emphasis on business in this book has been to supplement the knowledge that you have from other sources. I have not addressed editorial skills directly for two reasons:

1. Many other resources already exist to help you build editorial skills.
2. Editorial skills are far too broad to address all in a single book. The specific skills you require depend on the niche you have chosen for yourself.

All the same, this would be a good time to look back at your original goals, see if you have reached them, and figure out what you can do to improve if business has been slower than hoped. Remember that business plan you wrote back in chapter 4, "Getting Started"? Have you achieved the goals you set for yourself? If not, what might you do to increase the likelihood that clients will hire you? Maybe you need to improve the skills you started with. Depending on how much time has passed, maybe you need to update some of the skills you brought to your work—learn new methods for marking manuscript or new styles, for example. Or maybe you have reached your original objectives and are ready to stretch.

Whether you have fallen short of your initial goals or are ready to set new challenges for yourself, this chapter suggests ways for you to further develop your career. Read it for ideas, tap into other resources that can help, and build your skills and therefore your business.

Building Your Business

You might have started your business thinking small, with goals to get just a few jobs here and there. You might soon have found a passion for the business that you did not anticipate, however, leading you to want more. Working as an editor can be rewarding, and many of us develop the desire to dig in deeper once we begin.

Or, on a practical side, you might find that your financial needs have changed from when you started and that you *must* now accomplish more. Freelance editors lack the built-in salary increases that many employees enjoy, and the best ways to increase your income are to

1. work more hours and
2. acquire more skills to prepare yourself for higher-paying work.

The first of these possibilities depends on marketing yourself well, impressing your clients, and being willing to work long hours. Earlier chapters have offered strategies to help you in these areas. The second possibility requires improving and expanding on the skills you offer.

Whereas employees often find opportunities to learn from others in the workplace and grow on the job, those who are self-employed do not share these opportunities. Education and career growth for the home-based editor need to be self-motivated. Following are suggestions for expanding your skill set and improving your marketability.

Improving What You Have to Offer

In this section, I discuss building your skill set to augment the editorial services you already offer. In the next section, I discuss related businesses that might interest you.

Gaining Experience

If you find that you are not getting work and fear the old "need experience to get experience" handicap, figure out a way to get more experience. Experience does not need to be paid, and you will find many potential customers for volunteer assistance. Edit a church or a school newsletter or volunteer to work on the publications of other groups you belong to. If you don't find opportunities in your personal world, ask if you could help with the publication of a local nonprofit.

With so many people self-publishing now, authors everywhere need editors to review manuscripts. If you have a friend or a colleague with a manuscript in progress, offer to edit or proofread it. Beware: Prospective publishers often see through this type of experience when they notice a number of manuscripts with no publishers. All the same, you will be building experience, and some clients might consider this enough to give you a chance—or some particularly pleased recipient of your help might refer you later to a paying client. In any case, practice on manuscripts even without pay can help you develop your skills.

In addition to volunteer work, internships are sometimes available for those new to book publishing. While this does not fit the idea of a home-based business, you might acquire the extra experience and contacts you need to boost your business from home if you can manage to report at least part-time for a few months to a job in an office. Search "publishing internships" on the Internet, and see what comes up in your area. Alternatively, check the websites of known publishers in your region to see if they offer any information about potential internships. Even if your goal is eventually to work with other types of publications, experience in the office of a book publisher is invaluable.

If you land one of these internships, be proactive when you get there. Help as requested, but also take the initiative to jump into other tasks that interest you. Does a late introduction to a book need copyediting? Ask if you can help. Does jacket copy need proofreading? Volunteer your services. Those who see your willingness and ability will be more likely to contact you or refer you for other work after the internship ends.

Improving and Expanding Your Editorial Skill Set

If you are a self-taught proofreader or editor but have not been able to pass the publishing tests that lead to work, take the time to get some professional training.

A sharp eye for detail and a sound base in the language are good places to start, but they might not be enough if you haven't learned specific procedures and if you don't know when to make changes that could be discretionary. A small investment in even a short course can pay off quickly when you learn the conventions of the trade.

If you are getting some jobs but need more or better-paid work, what additional skills could you develop? Revisit the editorial tasks discussed in chapter 2, "Envisioning the Business." If you are a proofreader, maybe you could learn to copyedit. Copyeditors typically earn more per hour than proofreaders do, and the additional skills will set you up for more work. Likewise, developmental editors generally earn more than copyeditors do. If you are a copyeditor but find yourself frequently thinking about the overall structure of a publication and believe you have valuable suggestions to offer, consider developing your skills as a DE.

Are you really short on work and good at analyzing and organizing material? Consider developing skill as an indexer. Editors with this skill are in high demand, and if you learn to index well, you might better fill your calendar with work.

Advice from a Freelancer

"Proofreading and copyediting are skills, so learn them."—A Freelance Editor

Self-Teaching

How do you develop these skills if not on the job? No matter where you live, you can start with a book. Many editors are self-taught, and many instructional books are available. Often these books include exercises to help you practice and self-correct. See appendix C, "An Editor's Library," for suggestions. Also search online or in your local bookstore to find what's new on the market. By the time this book is published, more resources are likely to be available.

Following are brief descriptions of just a few books that I recommend, depending on the skills that interest you.

- Laura Anderson, *McGraw-Hill's Proofreading Handbook,* 2nd ed. (New York: McGraw-Hill, 2006). Anderson provides clear instruction for proofreading both print and web-based material. Intended for beginners and accomplished professionals alike, it also provides helpful resources for proofreaders.

- Amy Einsohn, *The Copyeditor's Handbook: A Guide for Book Publishing and Corporate Communications,* 3rd ed. (Berkeley: University of California Press, 2011). Einsohn's handbook serves as a practical manual for people just starting in the business as well as for experienced editors who want to sharpen their skills. It includes exercises with answer keys and detailed explanations.
- Scott Norton, *Developmental Editing: A Handbook for Freelancers, Authors, and Publishers* (Chicago: University of Chicago Press, 2011). Norton offers strategies for working with authors to develop manuscripts, mostly nonfiction publications. He covers the steps from shaping a proposal to executing a plan for development. Case studies from a variety of books and authors provide examples.
- Nancy C. Mulvany. *Indexing Books,* 2nd ed. (Chicago: University of Chicago Press, 2005). Mulvany explains indexing principles and practices relevant to authors and indexers alike. She gives practical advice and also presents perspective on the nature and purpose of indexes and their role in published works.

Attending Workshops and Courses

Ever heard of a publishing "degree"? Although some ambitious professionals benefit from a master's program in publishing, most start with a more general bachelor's degree, often but not always in English, journalism, creative writing, or communication studies. Continuing education courses in publishing and editing can provide you with specific skills, however, and are widely available, both on location and from afar.

If you have a university in your neighborhood, look for courses or even complete programs of study or certificate programs offered through its continuing education program. Appendix A lists a few such programs, or search the Internet for options in your geographical region. As one example, UC Berkeley Extension offers programs of study in both editing and technical communication (as well as in professional writing for those interested in a sidestep). If possible, find out something about the instructors so you can get a sense of their experience and orientation and see how their backgrounds match your goals. While certification is not required for individuals to work as editors, taking a course or a sequence of courses is a great way to learn new skills and practice the ones you already have. In addition, listing this accomplishment under education on your résumé will indicate to a potential client that you are serious about what you do and that you have invested time in sharpening your skills.

Editorial organizations often offer workshops that can be useful as well. Editcetera, based in Berkeley, offers programs in basic skills (such as proofreading, copyediting, and developmental editing), as well as programs focused on specific issues of importance to seasoned editors (such as editing with Word, editing for the web, or using English appropriately for a global audience). Editcetera also offers business programs for freelancers on topics such as career development, business management, and rate determination. Similar programs are offered by other organizations throughout the country. Think about areas of specialty that might appeal to you. In addition to courses with a focus on general skills, programs are available to help you learn how to edit medical content, technical materials, and memoirs, for example. See appendix A, "Resources for Editors," for some organizations that offer educational programs, or search the Internet for local groups.

Learning from a Distance

I recommend attending live workshops whenever possible; not only can you learn from other students as well as from the instructor, but you have the opportunity to network while improving your skills. If you are not in a position to attend a live program, however, check out the many distance learning programs available. Following are just a few examples of the types of programs that might help you improve skills from your home office itself. These are intended to illustrate possibilities. See appendix A, "Resources for Editors," or search the Internet for more possibilities.

- For full programs, check continuing education institutions such as UC Berkeley Extension. Berkeley offers its programs of study online, with instructors presenting over the Internet in scheduled sessions.

Getting It Right

"Times change, and freelancers need to have some awareness of trends, so they can adapt as needed," says one freelance editor. "The changes can affect tools, technologies, clients, whole industries, the economy, or 'public mood.' The awareness doesn't need to be obsessive, more an acknowledgment that the level of stability a freelancer wants in his/her life has to be created and maintained independently—and that means recognizing what's going on in the surrounding environment."

- For individual courses, try editorial groups such as Editcetera. Students may sign up for Editcetera's distance learning courses at any time and can complete the courses at their own pace.
- For short audio conferences and webinars on specific topics, *Copyediting* offers ninety-minute programs on topics ranging from editing figures and tables to writing headlines for the web. *Copyediting* also provides a PDF of course materials for all participants and offers CDs of programs for an additional fee.

For more information about these and other organizations that sponsor educational programs for editors, see appendix A, or search the Internet for programs in your region or programs to match your particular interests.

Expanding Your Clientele

Have you been limiting yourself to a particular type of client? Have you focused on book publishing specifically, for example? If you live in a university town, you might see if any professors or departments can use your help—with anything from scholarly manuscripts to research reports to course catalogs or programs for the arts.

No university nearby? Surely there's a hospital in your area. Does the hospital publish patient information? See if there's something you can help with. Or does a major retailer in your neighborhood publish catalogs that need editing and/or proofreading? This kind of work might not be intellectually stimulating, but working with sales material can carry its own interest.

For a review of potential clients, see chapter 2. Have you been overlooking an important source of work?

Increasing Your Technical Ability

Are you finding that your clients are unhappy with your estimates—or that they tend to disappear without offering you repeat work? It might be that you are working too slowly, and if so, you might increase your efficiency by improving your computer skills. As a copyeditor, could you learn more about Word to make it work better for you? Although the program is intuitive for beginners, you might learn some tricks to help you use it better. Do you know how to use tracking efficiently, effectively, and cleanly? Have you set up macros to automate some of the tedious and time-consuming tasks of editing? Look for a class in using Word to edit, or take a more general computer course to develop your skills. Alternatively, look for a self-help book on the topic, such as *Making Word Work for You: An Editor's Intro to the Tool of the Trade,* by Hilary Powers (Editorial Freelancers Association, 2009; updated edition expected 2013).

If you are a proofreader, do you know how to mark up PDFs using Acrobat? If not, find out how. If you are good at self-teaching, take a tutorial. If not, sign up for a course at a community college or elsewhere. You can use a free download of Acrobat to do some jobs, but other projects require a more advanced version. If you take a course, you might be able to get a student discount on the software, which will help offset the cost of the course.

Other computer programs vary in usefulness over time. For a while, some clients required mastery of Quark, and others required proficiency with FrameMaker. Now expertise with InDesign can sometimes boost an editor's chance of finding work. If you find that potential clients ask you about software products not in your toolkit, consider learning to use them. Again, adult education programs and community colleges are good places to learn these skills. Keep in mind that the software can be expensive, but balance this cost against the likelihood of increasing your workload.

Longtime editors sometimes get frustrated and even irritated by current demands that they have sharp computer skills. Any modern business requires most if not all workers to be computer proficient, however, and that can go for freelance workers as well. In addition to needing to mark up manuscript electronically, you might at times be expected to format a manuscript as part of your job—or you might qualify to work on more projects if you had that ability. Editors who have graduated relatively recently from college assume this responsibility without question. Those of us who were adults when the personal computer first emerged may still lack rudimentary skills, however. Don't make excuses if you are uncomfortable with a computer. *Get* comfortable. The more comfortable you are, the fewer problems you will have when working with clients and the more in demand you will be. No, you did not set out to be a computer pro, but in this age, essentially every professional must have expert skills on the machine.

Branching into New Territory

After you have reached your goals as a home-based editor, what if you want to expand your career even further? You can't move up as you might in an office, but if you have built a base of clients who trust you, you might challenge yourself by taking on new and more responsibilities. Besides adding editorial skills to your toolkit, consider branching out to new directions altogether.

Managing Subcontractors

One way to increase your responsibility is to manage and oversee the work of others. In this scenario, others would probably be independent freelancers like yourself. You might work as a project manager, overseeing the work of others for various tasks from copyediting to proofreading to indexing. Or you might work as a senior editor, farming out smaller pieces of a large project to others. Let your client know that you are doing this; a client who has hired you and trusts you might or might not be comfortable with someone else doing some of the work, and the client might need to pay other freelancers working on the project directly. Also check the quality of those working under you. Sloppy work from subcontractors will harm your personal reputation.

Teaching

Another way to branch out is to share your expertise with others through instruction. All of those continuing education programs mentioned earlier in this chapter need instructors. Especially if you have a graduate-level degree and/or prior teaching experience, consider inquiring about opportunities to teach.

Despite the expertise required for instructors of professionals, compensation is sometimes low. Known speakers with good reputations might also get assignments working in corporate settings for more respectable pay, however. Regardless, teaching can bring benefits beyond the paycheck in increased reputation and credibility. In addition, instructors have the opportunity to learn from others in their programs and to make connections that can be invaluable as they build a career.

Writing

Writing is not editing. It is related, however, and while any freelancer needs to be wary of the lines for any particular job assignment, some add variety to their career by crossing the border at appropriate times. In fact, some editors make a conscious transition into writing with the help of books, courses, and practice.

Strategies for Developing an Editorial Business

Improve Your Existing Skills	Build Experience	Improve Your Marketability	Branch Out with New Skills
Study a book	Volunteer for a nonprofit	Expand your editorial skill set	Manage other freelancers
Take a workshop	Work for an acquaintance	Increase your technical ability	Teach
Enroll in a distance learning program	Get an internship	Diversify your clientele	Write

Loving What You Do

People start home-based editorial businesses with all kinds of expectations and goals. The work can be hugely satisfying for those who master the skills and have the sense to manage their own business and provide the support their clients need. Editors can always find interest in what they do: No successful home-based editor should ever be bored. Dreading work each morning and watching the clock for the end of the workday are foreign to our routine. Furthermore, as an editor in charge of your own career, you have plenty of opportunity to grow as you like, to find new challenges every day, and to continue to provide meaningful service to the clients that interest you and that need what you have to offer.

San Francisco–based freelance editor Karen Seriguchi summed up her motivation for working independently thus: "It was a way to make money while I devoted my life to changing the world." Editors might not all be as idealistic as Karen is, but the ability to earn a living while doing something important and interesting is key for many. Remaining independent while doing that work adds yet another layer to the satisfaction.

Appendix A:
Resources for Editors

Organization fees are subject to change and are not guaranteed; they were current at the time of writing. Many of these organizations offer a variety of services, and many have resources available on their sites. Explore the sites for the latest information about all groups.

Organizations, Educational Resources, and Job Banks

American Copy Editors Society

website: www.copydesk.org
e-mail: info@copydesk.org
address: 7 Avenida Vista Grande, Suite B7 #467, Santa Fe, NM 87508
annual dues: $75 (student membership $40)
A professional organization working toward the advancement of copyeditors in newspapers, magazines, websites, and other journalistic endeavors. Resources, networking, professional development, a job board, and advocacy to promote the editing profession.

American Medical Writers Association

website: www.amwa.org
e-mail: amwa@amwa.org
address: 30 West Gude Drive, Suite 525, Rockville, MD 20850
phone: (240) 238-0940
annual dues: $160 (student membership $55)
Job leads, publications, networking, resources, programs; courses, certificate programs, and degree programs in medical editing and writing. See website for information about local chapters.

American Society for Indexing

website: www.asindexing.org

e-mail: info@asindexing.org

address: 10200 West 44th Avenue, Suite 304, Wheat Ridge, CO 80033

phone: (303) 463-2887

annual dues: $150

Directory of members, publications, resources, distance learning programs, jobs hotline. See website for information about local chapters.

American Society of Business Publication Editors

website: www.asbpe.org

e-mail: info@asbpe.org

address: 214 North Hale Street, Wheaton, IL 60187

phone: (630) 510-4588

annual dues: $40 to $100 ($50 for freelance members)

Professional association for full-time and freelance editors, writers, art directors, and designers employed in the business, trade, and specialty press. Newsletter, events, job bank, national conference, awards, educational resources. Free e-newsletter. See website for information about local chapters.

Author-Editor Clinic

website: www.authoreditorclinic.com

e-mail: info@authoreditorclinic.com

Instruction and mentoring for authors and freelance editors with a focus on developmental editing. Publications, resources, distance learning programs, blog.

Bay Area Editors' Forum

website: www.editorsforum.org

address: 268 Bush Street, No. 1900, San Francisco, CA 94104

annual dues: $25

Directory of members, job listings, editors' discussion group, resources, newsletter. Monthly programs open to nonmembers at no charge.

Copyediting

website: www.copyediting.com

email: info@copyediting.com

phone: (888) 303-2373

annual dues: $79 to $399, depending on level; some resources available for free

Blog, newsletter, educational programs. Also includes a searchable jobs board with free access.

Copyediting-L

website: www.copyediting-l.info

e-mail: iulist@iulist.indiana.edu

A worldwide discussion group of thousands of copyeditors "and other defenders of the English language" who want to discuss topics related to editing: style issues, philosophy of editing, specialized editing, reference books, client relations, Internet resources, electronic editing and software, freelance issues, and more. See the website for specific information about discussion group options and procedures for subscribing. Also a member directory, resources, and blogs.

Copyeditors' Knowledge Base

website: www.kokedit.com/ckb.php

phone: (631) 474-1170

Resource list published by Katharine O'Moore-Klopf. Links to hundreds of articles classified by category: the basics, education and certification, business tools, editing tools, networking, finding work, and profession-related reading.

Council of Science Editors

website: www.councilscienceeditors.org

e-mail: CSE@CouncilScienceEditors.org

address: 10200 West 44th Avenue, Suite 304, Wheat Ridge, CO 80033

phone: (720) 881-6046

annual dues: $179 (student membership $45, emeritus membership $82)

Networking, educational programs, gatherings, and job bank for science editors and writers.

Craigslist

website: www.craigslist.org

Job bank and more (community event announcements, volunteer opportunities, etc.). See "writing/editing" under "jobs."

Editcetera

website: www.editcetera.com

e-mail: info@editcetera.com

address: 2034 Blake Street, Suite 5, Berkeley, CA 94704

phone: (510) 849-1110

annual dues: $50 for applicants accepted for membership

Applications accepted from full-time freelance publishing professionals living in specific Northern California counties and having at least four years of experience in the business. Membership includes job referrals, networking, newsletter, resources. Workshops and distance learning programs available to nonmembers.

Editorial Freelancers Association

website: www.the-efa.org

e-mail: info@the-efa.org

address: 71 West 23rd Street, Fourth Floor, New York, NY 10010-4102

phone: (212) 929-5400

dues: $145 per year or $260 for two years, plus $35 enrollment fee for new members

Association of editors, writers, indexers, proofreaders, researchers, desktop publishers, translators, and others who offer a broad range of skills and specialties. Member directory, newsletter, networking programs, training and distance learning programs, discussion group, job list, information about and access to health insurance. See website for information about local chapters.

Editors' Association of Canada

website: www.editors.ca

annual dues: voting membership $257.50 + HST (harmonized sales tax); other options available

Membership directory, job leads, resources, programs, professional development. See website for information about local chapters.

Elance

website: www.elance.com

address: 441 Logue Avenue, Mountain View, CA 94043

phone: (650) 316-7500

annual dues: varies; see website for options

Online job leads for writers and other freelancers. Resources and tools.

Emerson College

website: www.emerson.edu

e-mail: continuing@emerson.edu

address: 120 Boylston Street, Boston, MA 02116

phone: (617) 824-8280

Certificate program in copyediting; nine modules required. Other professional studies programs include digital journalism, digital media production, literary publishing, and professional communication.

Freelancers Union

website: www.freelancersunion.org

address: 20 Jay Street, Suite 700, Brooklyn, NY 11201

Free to join. Union for independent workers of all kinds. Information about and access to health, dental, life, and disability insurance for independent workers; information about retirement plan for independent workers, networking, training, events, resources, advocacy. See website for information specific to your needs.

International Association of Business Communicators (IABC)

website: www.iabc.com

address: 601 Montgomery Street, Suite 1900, San Francisco, CA 94111

phone: (415) 544-4700 or (800) 776-4222

annual dues: varies (currently $259 to $324 in the United States, depending on chapter, plus $40 application fee; student discounts available)

Membership currently includes fifteen thousand business communications professionals from more than eighty countries. Resources, networking opportunities, job-searching assistance, and learning opportunities. See website for information about local chapters.

Media Alliance

website: www.media-alliance.org

e-mail: information@media-alliance.org

address: 1904 Franklin Street, Suite 818, Oakland, CA 94612

phone: (510) 684-6853

annual dues: varies; individual membership rates from $35 to $95

Membership open to all interested persons in publishing, journalism, writing, television, filmmaking, and related fields. Publications, workshops, job bank, special events, advocacy.

Media Bistro

website: www.mediabistro.com

address: 475 Park Avenue South, Fourth Floor, New York, NY 10016

phone: (212) 389-2000

annual dues: many benefits free; AvantGuild membership (with increased benefits) $55

Organization for anyone who creates or works with content: editors, writers, producers, designers, publishers, and production and circulation people. Networking, job bank, and more. Workshops and distance learning programs, including online certificate program in copyediting.

National Association for the Self-Employed

website: www.nase.org

address: PO Box 241, Annapolis Junction, MD 20701

phone: (800) 649-6273 (continental United States); (800) 232-6273 (residents of Alaska and Hawaii)

annual dues: $120 (student membership $25, veteran membership $99)

Benefits include access to tax and legal assistance, information about and access to discounted health and dental insurance, access to life insurance, printing services, credit cards, and more.

New York University School of Continuing and Professional Studies

website: www.scps.nyu.edu

e-mail: scps.info@nyu.edu

address: 7 East Twelfth Street., Room 133, New York, NY 10003

phone: (212) 998-7200

Certificate programs in editing, publishing, and digital publishing. Five courses required for each certificate.

Northwest Independent Editors Guild

website: www.edsguild.org

address: PO Box 1630, Snoqualmie, WA 98065

e-mail: info@edsguild.org

annual dues: $40

Regional alliance of professional freelance editors in the Pacific Northwest. Membership directory, resources, job postings, meetings, classes, and discussion group.

Publishers Marketplace

website: www.publishersmarketplace.com

monthly dues: $20 for full access to services and subscription to newsletter

A site for networking and finding clients; has web pages for member writers, agents, and authors. Free daily e-mail newsletter; expanded version for members. Free online job board and searching.

Publishing Professionals Network [formerly Bookbuilders West]

website: www.bookbuilders.org/wordpress

address: 9328 Elk Grove Boulevard, Suite 105-250, Elk Grove, CA 95624

e-mail: operations@bookbuilders.org

phone: (916) 320-0638

annual dues: varies, starting at $50 for one- or two-person companies accepted for membership

Membership by application and acceptance for firms and individuals in the book-publishing industry in thirteen western states, including single-person companies who provide editing, design, or production services to western publishers. Educational resources, a scholarship program, dinner events, social mixers, and an annual book show and awards. Free online job bank and industry-related news for members and nonmembers.

Society for Technical Communication

website: www.stc.org

e-mail: stc@stc.org

address: 9401 Lee Highway, Suite 300, Fairfax, VA 22031

phone: (703) 522-4114

annual dues: varies; basic membership starts at $225, plus $30 for new members.

Publications, networking, conferences and seminars, forums, job bank, and more. See website for information about local chapters.

Society of Professional Journalists

website: www.spj.org

address: Eugene S. Pulliam National Journalism Center, 3909 N. Meridian St., Indianapolis, IN 46208

phone: (317) 927-8000

annual dues: $75 for professionals; discounted fees for students and some others

Member directory, resources, training and distance learning programs, awards, job bank. See website for information about local chapters.

UC Berkeley Extension

website: www.unex.berkeley.edu

e-mail: info@unex.berkeley.edu

address: 1995 University Avenue, Suite 110, Berkeley, CA 94704

phone: (510) 642-4111

Courses in writing, editing, and technical communication. Four-course professional sequence in editing, available online or in person.

UC San Diego Extension

website: www.extension.ucsd.edu

e-mail: unex-reg@ucsd.edu

phone: (858) 534-3400

Courses in grammar and copyediting lead to a copyediting certificate; related courses in editing available, all online.

University of Chicago Graham School of Continuing Liberal and Professional Studies

website: www.grahamschool.uchicago.edu

e-mail: aneff@uchicago.edu

address: 1427 East Sixtieth Street, Chicago, IL 60637

phone: (773) 702-1682

Certificate program in editing; online certificate program in medical writing and editing.

University of Washington Professional and Continuing Education

website: www.pce.uw.edu

e-mail: info@pce.uw.edu

phone: (206) 685-8936 or (888) 469-6499

Certificate program in editing.

Women's National Book Association

website: www.wnba-books.org

e-mail: info@wnba-books.org

address: PO Box 237, FDR Station, New York, NY 10150

annual dues: $50

Membership open to all interested persons, male or female, in publishing, bookselling, libraries, writing, and other book-related fields: all women and men who work with and value books. The WNBA was established in 1917, before women in America had the right to vote. Networking, education, local chapter newsletter; national newsletter. See website for information about local chapters.

Publications

"Copyediting"

website: www.copyediting.com

Newsletter of Copyediting; formerly called "Copy Editor." Complimentary access to articles and blog posts. Membership starts at $79, depending on needs and access to newsletters and training opportunities.

Literary Market Place: The Directory of American Book Publishing (LMP)

website: www.literarymarketplace.com

e-mail: custserv@infotoday.com

phone: (800) 300-9868

Published annually by Information Today. Available at the reference desk of public libraries. Print copy $359. Also available online: annual subscription $399, weekly subscription $24.95, limited free access. Lists US and Canadian publishers, agents, trade events, awards, and more.

Publishers Weekly

website: www.publishersweekly.com

address: 71 West 23rd Street, #1608, New York, NY 10010

phone: (212) 377-5500

Subscriptions $249.99 per year for print and digital, $209 per year for digital only. Available in libraries. A weekly magazine about book publishing. Daily e-mail newsletter for subscribers.

Guidelines for Establishing Rates

Editorial Freelancers Association

website: www.the-efa.org/res/rates.php

A concise guide to typical fees and paces for freelance publishing tasks.

New Jersey Creatives Network

website: www.njcreatives.org/membership/120-how-much-should-i-charge.html

A comprehensive guide to rates for a variety of publishing tasks. Also includes introductory notes about setting rates within suggested ranges.

Editorial Skill	Description	Trade Publishing/ Nonprofit Rates	Corporate Rates	High-Tech Rates	Author Rates	Typical Pace
Proofreader	Checks final pages for errors in text and design	$20–40	$30–50	$40–60	$15–60	7–15 ms pages/hour
Copyeditor	Ensures correct use of language and consistent style—word for word and sentence for sentence	$25–45	$30–80	$40–85	$20–85	2–10 ms pages/hour
Editorial proofreader	Performs a combination of proofreading and light copyediting tasks	$25–45	$35–80	$40–85	$20–85	3–10 ms pages/hour
Substantive editor	Performs heavy-level copyediting tasks; rewrites for clarity and tone	$40–60	$45–100	$60–100	$35–100	2–5 ms pages/hour
Developmental editor	Works with the author on broad issues of content and organization	$45–60	$45–100	$75–100	$40–100	1–5 ms pages/hour
Technical editor	Ensures that difficult information is presented clearly; includes copyediting and/or developmental editing	$45–75	$60–100	$75–100	$40–100	1–10 ms pages/hour

Editorial Skill	Description	Trade Publishing/ Nonprofit Rates	Corporate Rates	High-Tech Rates	Author Rates	Typical Pace
Fiction editor	Works with creative manuscripts, taking care to maintain the author's style; includes copyediting and/or developmental editing	$25–45	NA	NA	$15–100	3–10 ms pages/hour
Web editor	Edits material for the web, utilizing knowl-edge of on-screen reading practices and search functions	$45–75	$55–100	$75–100	$40–100	1–10 ms pages/hour
Indexer	Creates an alphabeti-cal list of items within a text to help a reader navigate a publication	$4/page +	NA	NA	$2–12 /page $30–60 /hour	5–10 book pages/hour
Production editor	Manages publishing projects from manu-script to delivery of bound books	$45–60	$55–100	$75–100	$40–100	NA

Notes:

1. Rates here are based on surveys of freelance editors throughout the country, together with input from clients. Although ranges are broad, even these guidelines are not definitive; clients sometimes pay more or less, depending on (a) the complexity of the job, (b) the expertise/skill of the freelancer, (c) the ability of the client to pay, and (d) additional demands, such as rush or technical skill requirements. Rates at the high end or above the maximum noted here are usually possible only under special circumstances and/or for freelancers with rare skills.

2. Except for indexers (who always work with printed pages), paces are based on manuscript pages of 250 words. Paces can also fall outside of these ranges for manuscripts that are particularly well prepared or particularly problematic.

Appendix C: An Editor's Library

Listed here are just some of the resources most often recommended by and for editors. Because the business of publishing is always changing as technologies evolve, it is important to look for relatively current publications and for the latest editions.

Style Guides

American Medical Association Manual of Style: A Guide for Authors and Editors. 10th ed. New York: Oxford University Press, 2009.

The Associated Press Stylebook and Briefing on Media Law 2011. 45th ed. New York: Basic Books, 2011.

The Bluebook: A Uniform System of Citation. 19th ed. Cambridge, MA: Harvard Law Review Association, 2010.

The Chicago Manual of Style. 16th ed. Chicago: University of Chicago Press, 2010.

Microsoft Manual of Style. 4th ed. Redmond, WA: Microsoft Press, 2012.

MLA Style Manual and Guide to Scholarly Publishing. 3rd ed. New York: Modern Language Association of America, 2008.

New York Times Manual of Style and Usage: The Official Style Guide Used by the Writers and Editors of the World's Most Authoritative Newspaper. Rev. ed. Edited by Allan M. Siegal and William G. Connolly. New York: Three Rivers Press, 1999.

Publication Manual of the American Psychological Association. 6th ed. Washington, DC: APA, 2009.

Scientific Style and Format: The CSE Manual for Authors, Editors, and Publishers. 7th ed. Wheat Ridge, CO: Council of Science Editors, 2006.

US Government Printing Office Style Manual: An Official Guide to the Form and Style of Federal Government Printing. Washington, DC: US Government Printing Office, 2010.

Wired Style: Principles of English Usage in the Digital Age. Rev. ed. Edited by Constance Hale and Jessica Scanlon. New York: Broadway Books, 1999.

The Yahoo! Style Guide: The Ultimate Sourcebook for Writing, Editing, and Creating Content for the Digital World. New York: St. Martin's Griffin, 2010.

Dictionaries

American Heritage Dictionary of the English Language. 5th ed. Boston: Houghton Mifflin Harcourt, 2011.

Merriam-Webster's Collegiate Dictionary. 11th ed. Springfield, MA: Merriam-Webster, 2008.

Random House Webster's College Dictionary with CD Rom. Rev. ed. New York: Random House Reference, 2005.

Random House Webster's Unabridged Dictionary. 2nd ed. New York: Random House Reference, 2005.

Webster's Third New International Dictionary. Unabridged. Springfield, MA: Merriam-Webster, 2002.

Usage Guides

The American Heritage Guide to Contemporary Usage and Style. Boston: Houghton Mifflin Harcourt, 2005.

Bernstein, Theodore M. *The Careful Writer: A Modern Guide to English Usage.* New York: Free Press, 1995.

Burchfield, R. W. *Fowler's Modern English Usage.* Rev. 3rd ed. New York: Oxford University Press, 2004.

Fowler, H. W. *A Dictionary of Modern English Usage: The Classic First Edition.* New York: Oxford University Press, 2010.

Garner, Bryan A. *Garner's Modern American Usage.* 3rd ed. New York: Oxford University Press, 2009.

Maggio, Rosalie. *Talking about People: A Guide to Fair and Accurate Language.* 3rd ed. Westport, CT: Greenwood, 1997.

Merriam-Webster's Dictionary of English Usage. Springfield, MA: Merriam-Webster, 1994.

Basic Grammar Handbooks

Glenn, Cheryl, and Loretta Gray. *The Hodges Harbrace Handbook*. 18th ed. Boston: Wadsworth Publishing, 2012.

Huddleston, Rodney D., and Geoffrey K. Pullum. *The Cambridge Grammar of the English Language*. New York: Cambridge University Press, 2002.

Sabin, William A. Gregg *Reference Manual: A Manual of Style, Grammar, Usage, and Formatting*. 11th ed. Hoffman Estates, IL: Career Education, 2010.

Guides and Other Helpful Resources for Editors

Anderson, Laura Killen. *McGraw-Hill's Proofreading Handbook*. 2nd ed. New York: McGraw-Hill, 2006.

Cleveland, Donald B., and Ana D. Cleveland. *Introduction to Indexing and Abstracting*. 3rd ed. Englewood, CO: Libraries Unlimited, 2000.

The Copyeditor's Guide to Substance and Style. 3rd rev. ed. Alexandria, VA: EEI Press, 2006.

Einsohn, Amy. *The Copyeditor's Handbook: A Guide for Book Publishing and Corporate Communications*. 3rd ed. Berkeley, CA: University of California Press, 2011.

Krug, Steve. *Don't Make Me Think: A Common Sense Approach to Web Usability*. 2nd ed. Berkeley, CA: New Riders Publishing, 2006.

Mulvany, Nancy C. *Indexing Books*. 2nd ed. Chicago: University of Chicago Press, 2005.

Norton, Scott. *Developmental Editing: A Handbook for Freelancers, Authors, and Publishers*. Chicago: University of Chicago Press, 2011.

Powers, Hilary. *Making Word Work for You: An Editor's Intro to the Tool of the Trade*. New York: Editorial Freelancers Association, 2009. (*Making Word 2010 Work for You* expected 2013.)

Redish, Janice (Ginny). *Letting Go of the Words: Writing Web Content that Works*. 2nd ed. San Francisco: Morgan Kaufmann Publishers, 2012.

Ruby, Jennie. *Editing with Microsoft Word 2007, "Skills and Drills" Learning*. Riva, MD: IconLogic, 2009.

Saller, Carol Fisher. *The Subversive Copy Editor: Advice from Chicago (or, How to Negotiate Good Relationships with Your Writers, Your Colleagues, and Yourself)*. Chicago: University of Chicago Press, 2009.

Sharpe, Leslie T., and Irene Gunther. *Editing Fact and Fiction: A Concise Guide to Book Editing*. New York: Cambridge University Press, 1994.

Sjoholm, Barbara. *An Editor's Guide to Working with Authors.* Port Townsend, WA: Rainforest Press, 2010.

Smith, Peggy. *Mark My Words: Instruction and Practice in Proofreading.* 3rd ed. Alexandria, VA: EEI Press, 1997.

Stainton, Elsie Myers. *The Fine Art of Copyediting.* 2nd ed. New York: Columbia University Press, 2002.

Stauber, Do Mi. *Facing the Text: Content and Structure in Book Indexing.* Eugene, OR: Cedar Row Press, 2004.

Sullivan, K. D., and Merilee Eggleston. *The McGraw-Hill Desk Reference for Editors, Writers, and Proofreaders (with CD-ROM).* New York: McGraw-Hill, 2006.

Tarutz, Judith A. *Technical Editing: The Practical Guide for Editors and Writers.* New York: Perseus Books, 1992.

Turabian, Kate L. *A Manual for Writers of Research Papers, Theses, and Dissertations: Chicago Style for Students and Researchers.* Revised by Wayne C. Booth, Gregory G. Colomb, Joseph M. Williams, and University of Chicago Press editorial staff. 7th ed. Chicago: University of Chicago Press, 2007.

Williams, Joseph M., and Joseph Bizup. *Style: Lessons in Clarity and Grace.* 11th ed. New York: Longman, 2013.

Resources for Self-Employed Editors

Embree, Mary. *Starting Your Career as a Freelance Editor: A Guide to Working with Authors, Books, Newsletters, Magazines, Websites, and More.* New York: Allworth Press, 2012.

Goodman, Michelle. *My So-Called Freelance Life: How to Survive and Thrive as a Creative Professional for Hire.* Berkeley, CA: Seal Press, 2008.

Kamoroff, Bernard B., CPA. *Small Time Business Operator: How to Start Your Own Business, Keep Your Books, Pay Your Taxes and Stay Out of Trouble!* Willits, CA: Bell Springs Publishing, 2008.

Lonier, Terri. *Working Solo: The Real Guide to Freedom and Financial Success with Your Own Business.* 2nd ed. New York: Wiley, 1998.

Rogers, Trumbull. *Editorial Freelancing: A Practical Guide.* Bayside, NY: Aletheia Publications, 1995.

Zobel, Jan. *Minding Her Own Business.* 4th ed. Naperville, IL: Sphinx Publishing, 2005.

Websites Worth Bookmarking

Acronym Finder, www.AcronymFinder.com

American Psychological Association, www.apastyle.org

Associated Press Stylebook Online, www.apstylebook.com

Bartleby Library, www.bartleby.com

Full texts of many books online, including William Strunk's Elements of Style and a version of John Bartlett's Familiar Quotations

The Chicago Manual of Style, www.chicagomanualofstyle.org

Information about the 16th edition of Chicago Style, including Q&A and online search features

The Editorium, www.editorium.com

Macros (for a fee) to reduce the amount of time needed to do online editing in Microsoft Word; free newsletter

Grammar Hotline Directory, www.tcc.edu/students/resources/writcent/GH/hotlinol.htm

Contact information for grammar hotlines throughout the United States; maintained by the Tidewater Community College Writing Center

Grammar Resources on the Web, http://writing-program.uchicago.edu/resources/grammar.htm

Links to grammar and writing resources on the web; maintained by the University of Chicago Writing Program

HTML Goodies, www.htmlgoodies.com

Tutorials on HTML and creating websites

Infoplease, www.infoplease.com

A comprehensive reference source that combines the contents of an encyclopedia, a dictionary, an atlas, and several almanacs

International Trademark Association (INTA), www.inta.org

Internet Public Library. www.ipl.org

Library of Congress catalog, http://catalog.loc.gov

Lynda.com, www.lynda.com

Tutorials and instructions for learning to use software—thousands of videos covering hundreds of topics (membership $25 per month or $250 per year gives full access to materials)

Merriam-Webster Online, www.merriam-webster.com

Free; Online Webster's Third Unabridged also available for $29.95 per year, with a free fourteen-day trial available

Modern Language Association, www.mla.org

One Look, www.onelook.com

Search to many online dictionaries and acronym databases

Refdesk, www.refdesk.com

Indexes and reviews of information-based sites

Small Business Administration, www.sba.gov

TechWeb, www.techweb.com/encyclopedia

An encyclopedia of technical terms

US Government Agencies, www.firstgov.gov

Portal

US Government Printing Office, www.access.gpo.gov

Style manual

WhatIs, www.whatis.techtarget.com

Tech terms and acronyms

Index

O

Occupational Safety and Health Administration
  (OSHA), 48
offices, home
  advantages of, 42–43
  environmental conditions, 44, 46
  family life and boundaries at, 182–83
  furniture selection, 46–47
  insurance for, 67
  office equipment for, 49–53
  office space deductions, 103–5, 183
  references, 53–56
  start-up costs, 44, 45
  statistics of, 41–42
  workplace descriptions of, 41
  workspace selection, 43
  workstation ergonomics, 47–48
office supplies, 53
OSHA (Occupational Safety and Health
  Administration), 48

P

parenting
  boundary setting, 182–83
  day-care options, 185–89
  volunteerism, 184–85
  work-at-home advantages and disadvantages,
    43, 179–82
partnerships, 59, 60–61
patience, 15
payment collection, 92–93, 160, 170
PDFs, 51, 197
peace of proximity, as freelancing advantage, 43
Pernice, Kara, 140
personality, 146
phones, 52–53, 113–14
politics, office, 7
Powers, Hilary, 197
printers, 51–52
production editors, 21, 34
"Profit or Loss from Business" tax forms, 95–96,
  99–100

project assessments
  and declining jobs, 161, 162, 175
  disagreeable content, 161, 175
  rate estimates, 82–90
  subject matter and qualifications, 172, 174–75
project editors, 21, 35
project lists, 127
project management
  boundaries, setting, 160
  client communication and, 151–55, 157
  client dissatisfaction and problem solving, 158
  client expectations, 163–64
  client satisfaction, 131, 146–47, 164
  clients without computer skills, 162–63
  clients without ethics, 161
  flexibility and, 156–57
  independent authors as clients and, 158–59
  schedule and budget considerations, 155–56
  understanding requirements of, 148–51
  writing quality issues, 161–62
proofreaders, 20, 21–22
*Publication Manual of the American Psychology
  Association*, 13, 54
publications, technical, 38–39
publishers
  budgets of, 149
  conventions and style preferences of, 149
  as potential clients, 36–37

Q

questions (queries), 151–55
Quicken, 98

R

rates
  budgets impacting, 81, 149, 155, 160
  in contracts and agreements, 170, 171
  determining, 73–75, 78–81
  editorial skills and, 20–21
  ethics and, 177–78
  experience impacting, 80–81, 174–75
  project assessments and estimates, 82–90

About the Author

Barbara Fuller is the director of Editcetera, an association of freelance publishing professionals based in Berkeley, California. In that role, she manages a group of some one hundred freelance editors and writers who work with hundreds of clients, and she runs Editcetera's educational program, including both skills classes and business classes for editors. As a home-based editor herself on and off over the past two-and-a-half decades, Barbara has worked with clients including book publishers, university professors, independent authors, and a variety of journals and businesses. She has taught editing, writing, and business classes for editors for Editcetera, UC Berkeley Extension, UC Davis, and various government and private organizations. She lives in California with her husband and three children.